A LETTER TO HEAVEN

Part 1

"The Loss"

Disclaimer

I WANT IT TO BE KNOWN BY ALL that my intention in writing this book (and *including actual journal entries, letters and life experiences*) was and is, still, only to inspire, encourage and uplift others who might be going through similar circumstances, experiencing a loss of their own, whether from death, or divorce or abandonment. IT IS NOT my intention to harm **anyone** in anyway, to demean anyone or to commit any sort of libel or slander; but facts are facts, and the fact is, this is *not* a work of fiction – and life is not always pretty.

Any actual names used were used because these people were, or are still, family or friends, who have known as long as they have known me that I was writing a book, and were aware that they very well may be included in it one day; a few names may have been changed in instances where I did not have *specific verbal* or *reasonably implied* consent to include an individual in a book, and only they, themselves, and the people who know me, will know who these individuals are. It is not my desire to bring any harm to anyone, named or unnamed, personally or professionally. I only wish these individuals the best.

My honest hope is for the best blessings for everyone in the future; I have forgiven all, as I know I am on the right path now, and only hope others can forgive me for any pain I may have ever caused them. ~Sincerely, Dennel

TABLE OF CONTENTS

Pages

Acknowledgment

LeDon was so talented - she painted, she sewed, she quilted... she did needlepoint - and she could do any one of them, while reading a novel (and finish it all in a day). Yet she still managed to keep up on her bookkeeping business and part-time job... (even while struggling with her addition to alcohol). I don't know how she did it - but she definitely 'gave her all' to everything she did.

She left behind two small boys... Erik, who turned 6 two days after her death - and Kory, who was barely 2. I'm sure he hardly remembers her now.

She was older than I, by a year and a half - but married, and had children, much later in life. Anxious to go out and conquer the world, she grew up fast. Independent and defiant, she found her own way; although she got caught up in experimentation with drugs in her youth, ultimately, she did learn what was truly important in life.

She put so much of herself into everything she created... so much love, so much patience - and a tremendous amount of perfection. From the needlepoints that decorate my walls, to the delicate little stuffed bunnies, bears and cats she created, which now smile down upon me, every day, from my shelves. She left so much... in such a short time - you see, she didn't even get to turn 33.

So it is, to my only sister, LeDon, that I dedicate this book. She inspired me like no other - it is my hope, that in some small way, I too, can leave a part of me behind, by helping others, with my words. I don't know if I will ever touch as many lives, during my stay on this earth, as LeDon touched during hers - but I hope that, by sharing our lives and our experiences, with others, I will be able to touch a few, at least.

Thank you LeDon, for being as truly beautiful as you were - both inside and out.

***

Introduction

I had never really lost anyone close to me before... well - besides my grandpa, who died when I was 13 (and I simply distanced myself from that). I told my mom that I absolutely did not want to go to his funeral and she didn't make me go (thank God) - and thank you, Mom.

I never wanted anything to do with funerals... I always found them to be morbid and barbaric - all they accomplish is putting money in the pockets of businessmen, who enjoy preying upon the grief and guilt of loved ones left behind. Those who feel devastated, weak and lost (and are in no condition to make financial decisions), are told that they should want to 'give the best' to their loved one... the finest wood for his coffin, the finest silk for the lining - so it will last longer - but why?

Our bodies are made of the exact same substances that make up this Earth. Science has found practically every one of the chemicals that exist in our bodies, somewhere in the ground - so it seems obvious to me that we CAME from the earth to begin with, and therefore, we should go BACK into the earth when we die.

I always said, that when I died, I wanted to be cremated - no funeral, no big deal - just a simple prayer, and my ashes planted beneath a Weeping Willow tree (because I've always loved Weeping Willows)... and when others stop to admire the tree, they will feel my energy, for I will be there. But then, I will be everywhere - my spirit will be freed.

Don't get me wrong... I'm in no hurry to die - I love life. But I've always has this feeling that there was more to "me" than my physical being - that my body was simply a 'shell' or container, if you will. I have always been very aware of my 'inner self'. I truly believe our bodies were constructed for the sole purpose of 'housing' our soul while we are here on this Earth, and I'm quite sure our spirit doesn't care what happens to the container once we have left it. So, why then, do people so often feel compelled to 'hang on to' the bodies of loved ones (whether it be in a coffin, or an urn)? It's beyond my understanding.

I never saw the sense in painting a dead body, to make it look alive, and putting it in a fancy box, lined with silk or whatever, for people to look at one last time - just to place it in the ground where it will slowly mummify (because of the embalming process the grieving family agreed to pay for to keep their loved one preserved as long as possible) - and it seemed just as stupid to me to stick ashes on a shelf, to sit forever.

I want to get everything I can out of life while I am here... and leave everything behind, when I go. I cherish every single moment - good and bad - because we are only here for such a short time. That's the one thing I do know for sure... sometimes, life is way too short.

This, is my tribute, to my only sibling - my sister, LeDon - a beautiful woman, who was troubled at times, but who touched many lives and left them better for it... a mother of two, who didn't get to be on this Earth very long, but who's spirit is still very strong. I love you, LeDon.

***

FORWARD

After answering all those phone calls, I found myself wondering - if I should die, who would cry for me? LeDon had so many friends, and people who cared about her... the condolences came non-stop. And I had to wonder, because I don't associate with a whole lot of people. I mean, I have several friends - who I write to - special friendships that have developed over many years. Due to relocating, again and again, they have become 'long-distance' friendships... but life-long ones as well. I prefer to make friends for life, so I'm pretty choosy about whom I make friends with in the first place. I always joked that I liked animals more than I liked people, but in all honesty, it's true. Animals don't judge you or hold grudges. So I've always been hesitant to get close someone until I know them well.

My sister, on the other hand, loved people... all people, and she befriended everyone. She wanted to live BIG - and she did experience a good deal - (probably a lot more than she should have).

She wanted to be a star... she even modeled for a while - and she would do anything for anybody. Yes, to know her, was to love her.

But, despite the beautiful smile, and the positive energy which radiated from her - I have come to realize that LeDon was never, "truly" happy, here on Earth.

***

Chapter 1

FROM DENNY, WITH LOVE

"Jan. 4, 1996

Dear LeDon:

Tomorrow is your birthday, and I am dreading the day... you would have only been 33 - it's just not fair. Oh, how badly I wish you were here. I miss you so much, it hurts - and it's only been a week since you left us. I can't even concentrate on work. All I do is sit and think about you - about growing up (and growing apart)... and discovering a wonderful friendship in our adulthood - finally gaining that extra bond, of motherhood.

I still remember the first 'inkling' of mothering I saw in you - it was right after Brian was born. You flew down to see me... held him and looked at him, with 'that look' in your eyes, and cradling him close to your cheek, you said - "I don't know, what do you think?" - then you smiled... and quickly said "no, I don't think so", and you handed him back to me.

I knew your feelings would change, eventually - and when you finally became a mother, several years later, you were the most doting mother I had ever seen! Then, we gained a bond that we had never been able to share before, because you finally understood what I had always known - how wonderful the very basics of life were - what a miracle children are and what a gift motherhood could be... it was something you thought you never wanted, but found to be a beautiful thing.

I was watching our old home movies the other day, and of course, (you remember) - more than half of them are of you before I was even born. "LeDon, coming home from the hospital"... "LeDon, standing in her crib"... and so on. The first one of me, was at the age of 3 months - and in the next, I'm already a year! Of course, you're also in those with me.

But I understand why Mom and Dad couldn't resist filming you all the time... you always had star qualities. You were so precious and so pretty - you had that same sweet smile, and those great big dimples, that you still had as an adult. I always envied you for that - well, for a lot of things, actually. You were always prettier, smarter, stronger and more talented than me... you could play the piano with ease (while I struggled to follow the notes and make my hands work together) - you had a voice like an angel (and you weren't afraid to show it). I was so timid... I just couldn't - and still can't, really, sing - unless I'm alone in the car, or just in front of my kids. And then, sometimes, I think, I kind of sound like you.

Your skin was always perfect, and your hair, always beautiful... it grew four times faster than mine - and it seemed like you didn't even have to try - you were simply a natural beauty!

Now Mom tells me that YOU always thought that I was the special one... the smart one, the pretty one - that because I was smaller, more fragile, more delicate, you always felt that I was everyone's favorite. And I always believed you were so much better than me. I always looked up to you - and respected you - wanted to be more like you... but I never could, no matter how hard I tried.

Mom used to tell me that when they brought me into her hospital room, she told them they brought the wrong baby. There I was, bald and red-faced... but how? "LeDon was born with long, dark hair, and an olive complexion..". believe me, I had heard that more than once.

Yes, you were beautiful, right from the start - and so, you

deserved all those moments in the spotlight - all those home movies (and I am so grateful that I have them now). You were always the "star" of our family, and you always will be.

I honestly cannot bring myself to say that Mom and Dad went overboard...but... there are movies of your room, of your toys, and of all your little dresses, laid out neatly on display - reels marked "LeDon, outside of house 6-8-64" and then, "LeDon, outside of house 7-13-64", and so on.

There you are, dolled up in some adorable little dress... with your hair in the little 'cupie doll' curl that Mom always loved to put in our hair in, running down the sidewalk, smiling as usual (with your nose all wrinkled up), or playing in the grass, or picking flowers... oh, so beautiful. Oh, and then there's me - well, sort of - Mom's pregnant, and all dressed up for church, in a dress that matches yours.

Mom told me you were a little jealous of me, when I came along... though I don't understand why - perhaps, it was just because you finally realized the world didn't revolve around you alone. You always did like to be the center of everyone's attention - and I must admit, you were very good at it. Even on my first birthday, (I see from the old home movies) you had to steal the show - as, grinning ear to ear, you blew out my candle - then smiled for the camera!

Yes... most of our home movies ARE of you - and the rest capture our childhood together (camping, skiing, sight-seeing at Jamestown, Fredericksburg & Williamsburg - birthdays and Christmases, until we're about 7 or 8). Then, there are no more, except the few of the cats and kittens, who also shared our lives for all those years. We had so much fun growing up together, didn't we? We were given the absolute best - so many opportunities and experiences... and oh, how much we learned. With Dad in the military, we moved a lot - so friends came, and friends went - but we, always had each other... and even when we fought (as we often did, and as all siblings do), we never questioned our love for one another. I would have died for you, if need be - and I know you would have done the same for me. God, I miss you. I think about you every day... and I know I always will, until I see you again.

I worry about Erik and Kory, though - how are they going to grow up without you? Will they be ok? How will they know about you?? Why did you go? Damn, it's not right!

You know, Dad feels so guilty about what he did - for

kicking you out, when he moved Beth in - and for writing you/ us off like that. He regrets all the time he lost with you, as well he should... the time that he wasted, with both of us... he feels, somehow, that your death is his punishment. He has some absurd idea now that if he had just stayed OUT of our lives, had he not tried to contact us again that night, you might still be alive. He is carrying a heavy burden for the decisions he made twelve years ago. I wish I knew how to help him through it. He feels that he could have changed it all, I suppose, if he had not ever abandoned us - but that's not the way life works - things can't be changed. I'm glad we were at least able to get back in touch with him, before it was too late for you - I'm sure you are too.

   I told him he can't take the blame for this... nobody is to blame - except, maybe, the doctors - part of me thinks they should have caught this before it happened. It just doesn't seem like it was supposed to be.

   Just a few weeks ago, we were talking and laughing on the phone... so happy to have found Dad again - and you were fine! What happened? I wish I knew. But there are just no answers, it seems... no reasons - you're just gone.

Damn it, *LeDon... why are you gone?!?*

I wish you could tell us, somehow... what you know now. Well, maybe, some day, huh? I'm going to quit writing now - just wanted to wish you a Happy Birthday... and to tell you I was thinking of you. I miss you so much.

Love Always, Denny"

***

Chapter 2

THE PHONE CALL

I will never forget that awful day... it is forever etched in my mind - December 19, 1995 - the day I received the most horrifying phone call of my life. I was at cosmetology school, when Mom called to tell me that my sister, after having been in the hospital for a week, being treated for "dehydration", had just hemorrhaged in the brain, and was being rushed to emergency surgery. Mom was flying out immediately to Las Vegas, to be by LeDon's side.

I wanted to go too, but had to make arrangements first. I was terrified I was never going to see my sister again - just two days earlier, I had dreamed of her death... this, was all too real.

I got a ride home from school. No one thought I was in shape to drive... I made plans for my husband to take care of the animals (even though we were separated at this time), mapped a route to Vegas, grabbed all the kids, and drove fourteen hours straight through the night. I feared I was going to get there, just to be told that I was too late. But when I arrived, LeDon was drifting in and out of consciousness. They had relieved the pressure for the moment, but could not stop the bleeding. Half her head had been shaved and was terribly swollen and scarred from the surgery - she didn't even look like herself - she was yellow all over, and her face was so swollen... yet, she was still, so beautiful.

I held her hand, and talked to her... and for a brief moment, she looked at me. In that instant, she knew I was there - but then her eyes slowly rolled back into her head, and she was gone again. For two straight days, this was the ritual.

Then one night, as we all sat around her bed, watching her lay there - hoping for a miracle - she had an awful seizure. For five frightening minutes, we all froze, and waited, as her body stiffened and shook - arms stretched straight out, fists clenched tightly - and she moaned, uncontrollably. Her heart rate soared to 185 beats per minute, and we were all sure it was the end. Perhaps it would have been easier if it had been, for her... and for us.

But, instead, the week to follow was just a series of emotional ups and downs - as we all prayed for her recovery, struggled for strength, and tried helplessly to envision what the future was to hold.

LeDon had slipped into a coma at some point during the seizure that day, and she never woke up. We were prepared to spend the rest of our lives, if necessary, helping her to recover - but the doctors were not optimistic at all. They gave us NO hope. The clot on her brain had gotten so large, that it had permanently damaged the part of the brain that controlled waking... she would remain, for all intensive purposes, asleep to the world - she would never be able to talk again, or move - she had even lost the ability to swallow, or cough... and she was completely paralyzed on her right side.

We spent days and nights, watching... looking for any little sign of improvement, but no matter how much we hoped and prayed, or thought we saw, she only continued to get worse. The swelling increased with every CAT scan, and on December 27th, the doctor asked us for permission to remove her life support.

It was the hardest decision we ever had to make - letting her go. But I knew my sister - and LeDon would not have wanted to live like that... she loved expressing herself too much, and I believed, if any part of 'LeDon' remained trapped in that body, she would have gone stark-raving mad just laying there. So we chose to free her spirit. They expected that she would continue breathing on her own for a day or two - and when she stopped, they would not resuscitate her. And that's exactly how it happened.

How we wished we could help her, as she lay there gasping for air. Why couldn't they give her something to help her go - to make it easier on her? We do it for our animals. Why is it considered wrong, when a person is dying?

LeDon died, December 29th, 1995, at 1:30 a.m.

***

Chapter 3

THE AFTERMATH

We packed up all of her clothes and personal belongings - all
the things Felix didn't want to keep - along with all of her beautiful
tole paintings, needle-points, quilts and stuffed animals. We packed
it all up, and put it in a U-haul... and took it back to New Mexico. It
took some time to go through everything.

I kept her makeup, hair accessories, fingernail polishes and
perfumes - I use them every now and then - (although I was never a
girly girl, somehow, it makes me feel a little bit closer to her). She
had so many clothes, though, we just couldn't keep them all - she
probably never threw anything away. So we kept the 'special'
things, and what we each thought we could make use of (although
Mom doesn't think she can ever bring herself to wear any of it). I
was proud to wear her clothes, though, in her memory.

We donated the rest, so that someone else could make use of
it. But it was so hard, just dropping it off - 'dumping it', as if it
didn't matter. I came home and cried, just knowing that some

stranger would be going through it all, taking what they want, and never knowing what any of it meant to her. God, I miss her.

The months that followed, were the hardest ones of my life... I came closer to a complete and total breakdown, than I ever had before. Trying to put myself back together, was like trying to finish a jigsaw puzzle, with a giant piece that was missing. Nothing fit - nothing really, seemed to matter anymore... not like it used to. There were many times where I came close to losing it altogether... (and it is even more apparent to me now, reflecting back on it).

The problems Sid and I had been having, prior to LeDon's death, all seemed so menial now. So, together, we discovered what was really important... (that true love never dies) and we used what we learned through this tragedy to help strengthen our relationship. I honestly don't know if I could have made it through it all, without the support and complete understanding of my husband - in who's loving arms, at that time, I found solace - whenever I just needed to break down and cry. But at times, it wasn't easy... because the issues were still there to deal with:

"Mar. 8, 1996

Dear LeDon:

I hardly know what to do anymore - everything is so confusing right now. Sid wants me and the kids to move back in with him. But I'm so scared... I can't deal with him drinking - he gets so mean.

I have never felt so depressed... so devastated. I still can't believe you're gone. Life will never be the same again. Nothing is the same. When I got that phone call, my entire world started to crumble - everything around me seems to be falling to pieces, even still... what next? God, I'm afraid to ask.

I don't know how much more I can handle. I am actually beginning to understand why some people contemplate suicide... (although, I could never do it).

My children, alone, make life worth living and I'm grateful to have them. They need me right now, so I have to be strong for them. I want so much to watch them grow, and have kids of their own... so even if I had nothing else in this life to live for, I would live for them.

I'm worried about Mom tho - your death has also brought her

as far down as I have ever seen her. She is not herself - but, I
suppose - I am not myself, either. I love you, and miss you so.

Your sister, Dennel"

***

Death really puts things into perspective - what's important
and what's not. Life, really wasn't the same anymore. I couldn't
explain it - but, it just didn't have the same meaning. I went back to
school, and tried to pretend that I was alright... I needed to go, to try
to get my mind off of her - but I couldn't still - it just didn't work.
LeDon never left my thoughts. I did a lot of writing during this time
(mostly in notebooks) and found it to be very helpful.   I wanted
to talk about her - I needed to talk about her. Somehow, it helped
me to share things about her with anyone who would listen... my
friends at school, the stranger in the grocery store, the people at the
bank. LeDon was with me everywhere.

Mom, in contrast, found it easier NOT to talk about her... in
fact, for a very long time, she didn't talk about much of anything at
all. She went to work, spoiled her kitties and did her crafts
(sometimes, using LeDon's stuff)... but not really talking much - and
not at all, about LeDon.

I tried to be patient and considerate of Mom's feelings when I spoke about her. I never pressed the issue. We all have our own way of dealing with grief, I suppose... and who's to say what's right or what's wrong. What works for one, may not work for another, so we each just have to deal with things, in our own way, in our own time.

***

Chapter 4

FINDING FAITH

I have always done my best to see the positive side to every experience life has handed me (and believe me, I have my share of ups and downs) - and I trust that I have learned a valuable lesson from every one of them. Somehow, though, I failed to find anything positive about LeDon's death. All it really taught me, was how truly fragile life is, and how unpredictable - and that we should treasure it to the end... and be thankful for each day.

I find myself wondering a lot more about life now - about why we are here... and what we are 'supposed' to do - if there really is a purpose to life, or if we simply exist for God's enjoyment. Are we supposed to accomplish something here on Earth, or just appreciate it, for however long it lasts?

I questioned, at times, how God could "do" this - or how he could even "allow it" to happen. To take a young mother away from her two little children like that, it just wasn't right. But through all this, my faith did get stronger. I have come to realize, that God didn't "do" it... and he MUST "allow" it - because death, is part of life - it must be... and that's why were are here, to experience life, with all its ups and downs.

So I accepted it as it was, and my faith continued to grow; and my questions were eventually answered... in a subtle way, through the years. I came to the conclusion that, for the most part, God does NOT intervene. He watches, and perhaps, even prepares the way for us now and then. But when it comes to matters of life and death, God simply does not intercede - unless, of course, an individual has some extraordinary mission to fulfill.

Yes, even the good die young sometimes... maybe it would just be too difficult for God to try to save everybody that is "worthy" of saving... or maybe, he figured we would learn more, by simply letting nature take its course - death, after all, does not discriminate - and learning to deal with it makes us stronger. It could also be, that death is not such an awful thing (especially when it comes naturally) - and maybe even, just maybe - God takes the good specifically to free them from this world of pain.

Whatever the reason, life is, what it is... and things happen because of circumstance - cause and effect - (it's God's way of making the world go around) and I have learned that we do not control circumstance.

It was circumstance (a bad marriage my mother happened to be in at the time) that led LeDon to the streets, at the age of 13... and compelled her to experiment with drugs, alcohol and sex - and it was this rebellion, which led to her going to live with my Dad in California. We didn't see each other for several years after that.

It was those circumstances, that led her to a lifestyle that would ultimately destroy her - years of drinking, taking drugs, and abusing her body. And when we did meet again, she was not at all the LeDon I remembered. She told me that she'd had a "few" abortions... much to my horror - and it was strange how nonchalant she seemed about it all.

It was also circumstance (my father, marrying a girl LeDon's age) that caused her to leave Dad's when she was 18.

I still remember that day, as if it were yesterday. It was about one week before my first son was born (in May of 1983). I got a phone call from LeDon. She said that Dad had thrown her out of the house because she couldn't get along with Beth (the girl he married). I couldn't believe it at first - but when I got off the phone with her, I called Dad and he verified every thing. He said he didn't even want to discuss it... as far as he was concerned, he only had one daughter now. Well, in defense of my sister, I said, if he really felt that way, then he didn't have any - because LeDon was just as much a part of him as I was - and although we continued talking for a while, the conversation ended when he asked if I would "wait" and call him at work, to tell him when the baby was born, because Beth didn't like being reminded that he was going to be a grandpa! This hurt, because this was to be his FIRST GRANDCHILD and I had hoped he would be delighted to hear the news, whenever it arrived.

I made up my mind, right then, that I wasn't even going to bother calling him at all when the baby was born - and I didn't.

It was circumstance that forced me to speak to him, about a month after Brian was born. Mom was talking to him about LeDon's car insurance, when I happened to walk into her office. She asked him if he would like to talk to me... and then said, "well, here she is anyway". Begrudgingly, I took the phone. He simply asked if I had something to tell him. I asked if he really wanted to hear. "Sure," he said, so I told him he had a grandson, and his only response was "a boy, huh? -well."

After a moment of silence, I just handed the phone back to my mom... having received all the confirmation I needed that my dad really didn't care anymore - and I let it go.

I wrote him, a few times, in the years to follow... but never got an answer to one letter. We didn't talk for twelve long years.

I did, however, make it a point to stay in touch with my paternal grandma, and continued to let her know I was always open to hearing from Him if he ever cared to contact me. He was still my dad, after all - even if he had lost his mind for a while. I divorced, remarried, had two more children... and divorced, and married again - all without him even knowing.

It was circumstance that also brought LeDon and I back together with my dad after all those years. He and his then wife had filed for divorce, and he was going through some difficult times. He had called my mom for advice one night, and while he was on the phone with her, the police came to his door and arrested him!

My mom could hear everything as she was left hanging on the phone... apparently this woman had accused him of making harassing phone calls to her, and in New York (where they tend to side with mothers in divorce cases), he could be arrested for that.

My mom immediately called me…and that night turned my life upside down.

LeDon and I spent hours on the phone, talking about what to do - if we should do anything - Mom had a little money, I had just gotten my student loan check, and LeDon said she could come up with some but Felix didn't want her to help Dad because of the way he had treated her. She was still hurt by the things he had done, of course, and so was I - but he WAS our father... and we loved him, so ultimately, we decided that we were going to do whatever we could to help him.

Sid and I got in an awful fight after that call. He had been drinking quite a bit of beer while I was on the phone and got extremely upset about the conversation. Things just went from bad to worse, the minute I hung up, as he asked me, "Ya know, I know he's your dad an all, but really, what the fuck has he ever done for you?" Stunned, I replied "he raised me for the first twelve years of my life, and was a good father during that time!"

He stormed out of the room and things really got out of control. I'm not quite sure why, but before I knew it, Sid was coming back from the kitchen, with a butcher knife in his hands.

I stood there, frozen in fear, and amazement as I envisioned him lifting the knife behind his head to stab me - and he must have seen the fear in my eyes, because all the sudden, his fist opened and the knife fell to the floor. He began to sob, and said "what the hell am I doing?" And he reached out to me. I couldn't move, my arms down to my side, I just stood there as he tried to hug me. Then he let loose, still sobbing, "…now you can't even hold me."

I told him he had to leave. I couldn't live with that kind of anger, and we split up the next day. We rented a small house in town for him, and I moved in with my mom again. We let our mobile go back - a voluntary repossession. I put my horses on some friends' land and trusted them to care for them. They ended up being terribly neglected, and every thing just seemed to fall apart at the seems. It was only a few weeks later, I got that horrible phone call at school.

Once again, circumstance had placed me in a situation that I had absolutely no control over - a situation, that I definitely did not want to be in - and I was put on the longest emotional roller-coaster ride, of my entire life. I was not prepared for this. But then, I don't know how you can ever be - it's hard to lose someone, even when you expect it - it always hurts. But this, this was harder than anything I had ever been through before.

I still feel LeDon's presence, but I know she is "gone". We are here, and she no longer is. We watched her body deteriorate - but as things physically shut down, there was another part of her that seemed to leave, long before her last breath.

So is this physical world all there is? I emphatically think, not. I feel so much more around me than the things I see. There is an energy - not physical, but very strong and very real - so the question becomes, where DO we GO from here? If LeDon is really as close I think, then, is there truly a "Heaven"? How can she be both here, spiritually, and there? I know, what I know in my heart... the only thing I don't know is how to make it sound rational.

For eons, people have wondered whether a part of us goes on existing after the death of the physical body or not - they have imagined a spiritual plain - and for centuries, at least, man's imaginings have become reality... like going to the moon, or technology advances. It only makes sense to believe that we, as human beings, have some kind of insight that we, ourselves, are not even aware of. Maybe that insight comes from God.

One thing I have realized in recent years, is that I am still learning everyday. This life never ceases to amaze me. We never do, and never will 'know it all'... we can't, no matter how much we learn - this Earth simply holds too many mysteries - the universe, too much magic. There is simply too much knowledge out there for any one person to ever, even hope to learn in one lifetime. All we can do, is soak up as much as possible, while we are here... and enjoy life while we can, because it is often too short, and much too fragile.

I most definitely believe in a greater power (whether you want to call it God, or not, makes no difference to me)... I've never cared much for 'classifications' or 'labels'. It is merely one of the many mysteries of life - how the 'forces of nature', or fate, if you will, works. But no matter how you refer to it, if you remain willing to learn from it, you *will* benefit in the end.

One month after LeDon's death, it was also circumstance - my dad's job relocating him from New York to Texas - that gave us all the opportunity for another fresh start.

Mom, desperately looking for a change in scenery (and needing some diversion) decided to follow my dad to Texas. She and her husband, Al, owned their own construction company and

New Mexico had done nothing for it. So she asked me to help her move, which gave me to opportunity to look it over for myself, and even though I had previously looked in the atlas, only weeks before, at the maze of highways and roadways running throughout and all around the "metroplex", known as Dallas/Fort Worth - and told her "gee, I'm really gonna miss you, Mom" (because I never could have imagined living there in the middle of all that mess), it took me only a week to fall in love with the small town of Mansfield, just below that horrible maze of roads.

Sid agreed to come with me - to help me move - and was certain he was going to hate it. But it took just a week for him, as well, to fall in love with the beauty of the landscape. It was green - it was gorgeous - and it was warm... oh so warm. We were finally "home"... I could feel it in my heart.

"Aug. 20, 1996

Dear LeDon:

As I sit here tonight, in Texas, exhausted from our move, all I can do is think about you. You were probably laughing hysterically when Sid's car came off the tow dolly in the mountains of Ruidoso, two hours into our trip, without us even knowing it (because he forgot to hook up the safety chains). We backtracked an hour and a half before we found it! It had rolled down a gently sloping hillside, through a chain link fence - under the top rail - and came to rest on a stump, which took out the oil pan. Otherwise, intact, except for the things that someone decided to steal out of it before we got back there. I was so upset that all of your fingernail stuff was gone! Nothing else really even mattered to me.

It's been almost eight months, yet it seems like just yesterday - and at the same time, it still doesn't seem real. You're *not gone...* you can't be gone. How can you be gone? I still *feel you* all the time - and so does Kasey.

She told me, as we were driving down the road the other day, that you touched her arm. Just out of the blue. I was surprised, because you hadn't even been the topic of conversation at the moment - in fact, as I recall, we were singing. When all of the sudden, she got quiet, and then exclaimed from the back seat, "Mom, Aunt LeDon just reached down and touched my arm!"

I know five-year-olds can have active imaginations, but where did that come from, if not from you? It must have been you...

I have no reason to doubt her.

I should be tired after driving 21 straight hours, with the kids, the dogs, the cats (and the parrot and iguana) - all in the Suburban... Lord knows, the horses were never so happy as they were to get out of that trailer and see the long, green grass in the pasture. But I'm not tired... my mind is reeling - I think you would like it here. Mansfield is a pretty little town.

We're on 5 acres - and the house is beautiful... too bad it's just a rental. A little old lady owns it - she doesn't want to live in it - but she doesn't want to sell it either. She says we can stay as long as we want, so that's cool. Maybe, in a couple of years, when our credit is good enough to get a home loan, she'll be ready to sell.

Well, I feel at home here, for now, at least; and it's a nice feeling. I guess I'm going to try to get some sleep now. I'm sure I'll see you in my dreams.

Love, Denny"

***

Chapter 5

A GIFT FROM HEAVEN

I intended to get right back to school, as soon as we got settled - even transferred all my hours from New Mexico. I had earned over half of the credits I needed to get my cosmetology license, and had thoughts of owning my own small, beauty shop someday - or a mobile nail business. I was determined not to let all those hours go to waste.

But sometimes, no matter how determined you are, if something is not meant to be, it won't be.

One thing after another prevented me from getting enrolled back in school. After transferring my hours, which took over a month, I had to check out the schools - they were all so far away. I finally found one and made it out for an interview. And I was going to enroll there... was just waiting on my transfer letter.

But, fate had other plans for me... my mom got a job managing a small Law Office, which was in desperate need of direction - and it turned out that they were also in need of a skilled paralegal. Since I had thirteen years experience in this field, Mom asked me to take the job.

So, once again, I raised my glass to circumstance. She needed my help, and we could use the money... so I got a job that I didn't really want. At first, it was only going to be for a week or so - then a week turned into a month, and a month turned into six, which, before I realized it, turned into more than a year. Funny how that happens - how time gets away from you.

How I hated being confined like that all day, staring at those four walls around me, practically glued to a chair (except for the occasional walk to the copy or file room)... I hated the whole routine - from the drive in every morning, to the drive home every night.

Day after day, dealing with so many other people's problems - as if I didn't have enough of my own. It seemed like life was just passing me by as I sat there. Dealing with divorce, child support, custody battles and property disputes... why couldn't everyone just get along?

By the time I was finally ready to quit... or rather, by the time I finally convinced every one else that I was ready to quit, I had lost all my hours from school. Even though my hours were accredited when I transferred them, I found out (a little too late) that I had to actually re-enroll in school within one year of my transfer to keep those hours. It was late September, 1997, now - just over a year - and there was nothing I could do about it... except to start all over. And I just didn't have it in me.

The time and cost involved, just didn't seem worth it - and it wasn't what I 'really' wanted to do for a living anyway, so I decided to let it go. My cosmetology skills, it seemed, would have to remain of use only for my family.

But it was just as well you see, because fate had another surprise in store for me... that November, I became very ill.

I thought I had been going through early menopause for a while now. For two years, I had just been feeling 'out of wack' - probably from the devastation of losing LeDon - but whatever the reason, my body just wasn't functioning right. I was tired all the time... and cranky. I was becoming short-tempered and had a lot of headaches (generally, just feeling like shit). Then I got really sick... throwing up constantly, sick. I was extremely weak and had absolutely no energy whatsoever.

I finally asked a friend to take me to the doctor.

The doctor ran all kinds of blood tests to determine what was wrong with me and said he'd let me know. Much to my surprise, there was really nothing wrong... nothing at all.

It was all right, in fact – strangely, perfectly right:

"Dec. 15, 1997

Hey Sis...

I can't believe it! After seven long years, I am pregnant again! I feel your hand in this, somehow. Thank you.

I thought it would never happen to me again... I had given up hope of ever giving Sid a child of his own. This is truly a blessing.

This bundle of life now growing inside me... it fills me with such joy - such happiness, I can't even explain.

Yet, at the same time, it scares me a little bit.

I'm afraid of losing the baby again... I'm trying not to get too attached yet, at least, not until I past the first three months - both the others miscarried in the first trimester, so if we get past that, I will feel much, much better.

Kasey is so excited. I had to warn her that there is a chance the baby won't make it. I guess we're as prepared as we can be.

Well, I should go put my feet up - the doctor told me to take it easy. I love you so much! Denny"

***

The baby grew, and got stronger each day... and eventually I passed the three-month mark – no longer worried about miscarrying, and got over being sick. We had an early sonogram done because they were keeping a close eye on the baby.

We found out it was a boy, and even though Kasey always wanted a little sister, she was elated seeing the ultrasound - just knowing it was real. She was finally going to be a big sister! It didn't really matter what sex the baby was.

Of course, Sid was tickled that it was a boy. This was *his* first baby.

"April 1, 1998

Dear LeDon:

Well, since we found out the baby is a boy, I asked Sid if I could name him Kristofer (like I wanted to name Brian, almost fifteen years ago). Sid said he didn't care what I named him, as long as his middle name is Thomas... so that's it: Kristofer Thomas Tyon.

We found out, though, that he has the same condition Kody had when he was born, the craniosynostosis. It was apparent from the sonogram that the sagittal suture line in his skull is already fused - so he has no soft spot and that means surgery for this baby as well.

Sometimes, I have to question why God does things like this to me. Seems as though He gets a kick out of testing me - throwing stumbling blocks in my way just to watch me try to overcome them. But then, I guess, that's what He does, to everyone. I'm not any more, or less, special... it's just my particular set of circumstances that sets me apart from the rest.

I woke up this morning remember that today was your wedding anniversary. Nine years ago today, I stood by your side, as you and Felix said your vows.

You were so beautiful, as you walked around the pool and through the archway, which we had decorated in purple flowers (your favorite color)... Brian was in a purple shirt and Kody, just a baby, in a little purple jacket - you were the only one in white.

Wow, time really does go by too fast. Now, here I sit, pregnant with my fourth child - wondering if he was meant to be yours. I promise, I'll take good care of him.

You know how much I wanted another baby. Thanks for putting in a good word for me. I love you!

Forever, Dennel"

***

He wanted to wait... but on July 1st, 1998, at 7:00 a.m., my doctor induced labor- and at 6:46 p.m., Kristofer Thomas Tyon made his entrance into this world (and boy was he mad). Sure enough, it was obvious... his skull was fused solid as could be - he had a very long head, with a visible ridge from front to back - but he was absolutely beautiful to me.

Kasey was so proud to finally be a big sister. She was with me through the entire birth. She said it was the greatest experience of her whole life (which, at seven, seems like an eternity).

The birth of a new life is such a beautiful thing to be able to witness, and to be able to share it with her was wonderful. You just have to get past the 'physical' side of it - the blood and the view - and accept it for what it is... nothing short of a miracle. This little tiny being comes to life right before your eyes. As they cut the cord, and it begins to breath on its own, you can't help but feel blessed just to be there to see it. It was really neat to have her be a part of it and

I was glad that she wanted to be - and she was impressed to know that it could all be done with no pain medication whatsoever.

It really didn't seem to take that long.... only the last couple of hours were difficult. Sid was funny, because he was so excited. He was nervous, and afraid that he wouldn't know what to do when the time came - he just kept smiling at me the whole time - and that's really all he needed to do. I knew everything else would take care of itself. When the baby was ready, it would come - it just happens that way. As with all things in life, nature takes it course. We just have to follow its lead.

If we bear the pain, through the hard times, and do our fair share of the labor... staying focused and strong, and trusting that every thing that happens, happens for the best - we reap the rewards of our hard work, are blessed to experience the joy of love, and to gain knowledge from life's many lessons.

No matter how many times I do it, giving birth always amazes me... and it had been so long since I had held a tiny little newborn, I had almost forgotten how good it felt. I held him endlessly, at first, never wanting to put him down.

He would lay on my chest so comfortably, that I found

myself allowing him to just fall asleep there, and most of the time we would sleep the whole night that way.

Every one of my children have been such a blessing in my life... but this one, he was extra-special – somehow, I knew it right from the start.

***

Chapter 6

ANOTHER BUMP IN THE ROAD

In August of 1998, just one month and a few days after Kristofer's birth, my oldest son, Brian (now 15) fell and broke his hip, rollerblading - jumping a 5ft ramp... well, landing, actually. He snapped his thighbone, right off the ball joint. The doctor said it was an injury like that seen in an 80-year old man. He had to have it put back together with two steel pins.

When Bri first came out of surgery, he was medicated constantly... but he was in immense pain. Luckily, he slept through most of it. The second day was the hardest, because after he started coming out of the anesthesia, and the reality of what he had actually done, finally hit him... he realized the entire course of his life had just been drastically changed.

The doctor told us that he would probably never be able to skate again - or do anything that would risk injuring that hip in the future. He gave Brian less than a 50% chance that the ball joint would even survive this injury, but said we wouldn't know for sure, for two years. So, his dreams of becoming a 'freestyle' skating champion would have to remain just that - a dream.

We had a couple of peaceful months, with lots of time for Bri to reflect upon where his life was now headed. He was in a wheelchair for several weeks and on crutches after that, for two months. He spent the first semester of High School "homebound" teaching, with me - and then, just after he got back on his feet again, we hit another bump in the road.

Brian had finally started back in school. It was Friday, November 13th... I will never forget that date. Brian came home not feeling well (stomach pains again). He had suffered for the past three years with extreme pains in his stomach that no one had been able to diagnose... but this time, it was much worse. He said he had been jumping around in mud puddles after school and thought maybe he had just over done it.

He was soaking wet when he came in, and chilled, so I had him change clothes and built a fire in the fireplace for him. He laid down in front of it, with blankets on, and went to sleep. Later that night, he started heaving... over and over - and he was burning up with a fever.

I tried to take him to the doctor right then, but he refused, insisting that he would be ok. Finally, at 10pm, he told me he wanted to go. We took him to the hospital... and though they still weren't sure, they said everything was pointing to a burst appendix. So they took him in for exploratory surgery, just minutes after midnight.

"Nov. 14, 1998

Oh LeDon...

I came so close to losing Brian last night! Those moments, where we weren't sure whether he was going to make it or not, were the worst. The surgeon said that when he opened him up, his appendix was "floating in a sea of puss" and that Brian would not have made it through the night, had they not gone in there.

For a while, I felt like I was reliving the events of your death - and that made it seem all the more real. Knowing how fast it can happen - how quickly things can change - I was actually prepared for the worst.

Remember Brian being in the hospital three years ago, for this very same thing? They were going to do the appendectomy then

- had him scheduled for surgery and everything. He spent the night at the hospital... and half an hour before surgery then ran another test, told us everything was back to normal and sent us home! I cursed them for that then, and I do even more now. Brian should not have had to suffer all those years when it could have been take care of so long ago.

The doctors say he's going to be alright now. Though he has an awful open wound down the middle of his belly. They said he was so infected that they couldn't stitch him up - it has to heal as it is. We have to change the bandage twice a day, for three weeks, after we get him home.

Looks like we will be commuting between hospitals for the last few days of Brian's stay. Kristofer's surgery is scheduled for November 19th. Keep an eye on him for me, alright?

I love you.

Love Denny"

***

I went straight from Brian's hospital room to Kristofer's, for his skull surgery (known as a craniotomy). Since it was the second time I had been through this surgery, I wasn't too worried.

Though it's never easy, letting your child go when you know someone is going to be cutting into them - I didn't have a choice. Kristofer needed this surgery. He probably wouldn't have survived long without it. His skull had prematurely fused in the womb from this strange genetic mutation that seems to have occurred in my DNA. There was no room to allow for brain growth and that's all there was to it.

We were told it was a 'fluke of nature', when it happened with Kody... but in the past eleven years, they discovered a lot about it and turns out, it's a genetic condition, and each child of mine has had a 50/50 chance of this occurrence.

Sid and I both cried as they carried him away to the operating room - so tiny, so helpless - so fragile... it would be a heart-wrenching three hours before the surgeon came to tell us that all went well. They called up to the waiting room a couple of times to let us know how things were doing during the surgery, but we didn't feel better until it was all over.

The surgery had been refined quite a bit since 1987 - Kody's surgeon simply removed a 2"x4" rectangle piece of bone from the top of his skull, sent him home and told us not to drop him on his head. But Kristofer's surgeon cut a pie-shaped piece off the top, cut the back into 1" strips, left a few out, completely reshaped his head and pieced it back together again. Other than the stitches and the swelling, his head looked almost perfectly normal immediately after surgery. It was really amazing.

He was in quite a bit of pain for the first few days, and we felt so guilty, just wondering what he must have been thinking... last he remembered, we were handing him off to some strangers - and then he woke up feeling like this! He was probably really mad at us. His face was swollen to the point that he couldn't open his eyes, and his skin had a greenish-purple tone.

We spent 5 days in the hospital with him - took Brian home during that time. I stayed in the bed with him, and they fed me, because I was nursing him. That was nice.

Needless to say, I hope I don't have to see another hospital for a very long time. But I thank God every day for all of the surgeons, doctors and nurses who cared for my children during this time. I was glad to have all of my kids healthy, and home again.

***

Chapter 7

WHERE DOES THE TIME GO?

Things were finally getting back to 'normal' (whatever that is), and another Christmas was just around the corner. This year, it was full of mixed emotions... I was thankful my children were all well now, but I still missed LeDon so much, and this time of year, it seemed, would always bring up those awful memories of her death. This would be the third year, yet it still hurt as if it were yesterday:

"Dec. 29, 1998

Dear LeDon:

On this, the third anniversary of your death, I struggle to remember my many blessings, although they are evident. The pain is just still so raw – and I wonder if it will ever go away. I know they say time heals all wounds... but, at times like this, I find it hard to believe. I am going to miss you forever.

We managed to get through another Christmas without you. It just isn't the same though. But we have to keep our traditions alive, no matter how hard it is. Having Kris this year actually made it more bearable. Even though he had no idea what was going on, just knowing we have his whole childhood to look forward to made it easier. His hair is already growing back and his scar is barely visible. It isn't nearly as long or wide as Kody's - his goes from one ear to the other. Kristofer's is more than an inch above each ear and much thinner.

Brian is all healed up now too... pretty big scar though. He seems more focused on his future and has started writing poetry. I think coming so close to death was an eye-opening experience for him. He appreciates his life more now and isn't taking anything for granted.

I'm not either...

Wishing you were here, Love Denny"

***

So far this year, we had only had to deal with a variety of colds, flu, earaches, etc... then, I was sick for two straight months with a lingering, cold-flu, viral infection.

"April 20, 1999

Hi Donny:

I've spent the past two weeks in bed most of the time, but you know, even when I NEED to, it's hard to do. Brian has been able to avoid getting sick, I guess because he is gone so much between school, work and friends now.

Kristofer still doesn't sleep through the night... he always wakes up at least once or twice. Sometimes it is easier to just stay awake at night, when he is having a rough time. Then I just get things done that I don't have time to do during the day. He is constantly on the go now... almost walking and not quite 10 months old yet! So I can't leave him alone for a minute!

I barely get done when absolutely has to get done each day... animals fed, a few dishes done, maybe a load of laundry, etc. I have finally gotten most of the garden planted... a month or more behind schedule for Texas. It has been so warm here for so long already!

I will be getting a new baby in just a few more weeks... I bought a mare in October; she is purebred Quarter Horse, bred to a Paint Stallion. I am hoping for a little filly... I still have my hands full with Prince, and do not want to deal with another male! I have wanted another horse ever since Mishka died December '97, but I wanted a young filly and they are hard to find. Then last September '98, Kasey's pony got out on the road, and got hit by a van and died, so when I found this mare I thought maybe she might work out well for Kasey, and I could raise and train the baby... (you know, with all my spare time, haha).

I should quit now and go get something else done. I love you.

Always and Forever, Denny"

***

Sometimes, its easier just to stay up at night, to get all the things done that I can't get done during the day when everyone is awake. I swear, there aren't nearly enough hours in the day. Days turn into nights, that turn into days again, and the months begin to blur together:

"May 15, 1999

Hey there...

Where does the time go? How do months go by without me even realizing it? I've been pretty busy - as I'm sure you know - but it seems I barely get done what absolutely has to be done each day...

errands run, animals fed, a few dishes washed, and maybe a load of laundry here and there, but not much else.

Thankfully, the kids have remained healthy thus far, this year - except for the usual (colds, flu, ear aches, etc.) I was sick though, for two straight months - that lingering, combination cold-flu, viral infection. I spent two weeks in bed in February... well, as much as I could, with Kristofer crawling at top speed now.

He's almost walking. He's into everything, and *still* not sleeping through the night. He is always waking at least once or twice, just needing to be consoled. So he usually ends up sleeping in our bed - but that's ok.

Summer snuck up on me and as usual, I was not as prepared as I had hoped to be. I got most of the garden planted... but I was almost two months behind for Texas planting.

It's been so warm, for so long already! I absolutely love the weather here. We didn't even reach freezing last winter and it only snowed once. You would like it here.

Missy is going to have her baby here in a couple more weeks - I sure hope it's a filly. After raising two stallions, I don't think I want to do it again - so I'll probably sell it if it's a boy. I still have my hands full with Prince (and he's six years old now). I shutter to think what he would be like if I hadn't had him gelded as a yearling.

You know I've wanted another horse ever since Mishka died, so when Kasey's pony got out on the road and was hit by that van... and I found Missy, already pregnant, well - I saw fate at work again. I figured she'll be easy for Kasey to ride and, hopefully, the baby will be female so I could raise and train her for myself.

Mishka was 19 when I bought her, you know, and I had her for seven years... her death was not totally unexpected, but it was still hard to accept. It was especially difficult on Prince, since they had never been apart. That was his mamma. He stayed by her graveside, in the back of the pasture, for weeks.

That's when I decided I wanted another young one, so I wouldn't have to go through that again any time soon. It's just never easy to lose someone you love.

Brian is about to turn 16. I spent three months getting him to and from driving school, in addition to everything else I've been doing. It will be so nice when he finally gets his license! Mom is giving him the Grand Prix (the one I bought when I was pregnant with him, and sold to her when I left Mont). He thinks it's pretty cool that it's always been in the family and it's his exact age. Mom calls her "Old Blue" and she's having it painted for him. I don't think it'll hold up a lot longer, but it's a good starter car for him.

Well, I've got to go... I need to run some errands and do birthday shopping. I'll write again soon, tho.

Wish you could write back.

All my Love, Dennel"

***

I don't think there could ever be enough hours in the day. The summer disappeared as quickly as it came. As the flowers withered and the leaves began to fall, I felt as though I was losing my grip on things. I was losing control. The year was almost over, once again - and I felt like I hadn't accomplished anything. There was still so much left to do.

I wasn't sure I was ready for the holidays to begin again already. Seems they come faster every single year. I remember, when we were young, it used to take forever for Christmas to come around again. Now there aren't enough days in the year! I start dreading it about mid-October, when the stores all start stocking their shelves with garland and ornaments and those musical Santas.

It just annoys me. They should let Halloween get over with first.

LeDon loved Halloween. She went to so much work to make the most extravagant costumes... a Snow White dress (which I now have), a 50's Flapper, a princess, a bunch of grapes (when she was pregnant) - and for the kids, a squirrel, an elephant, a dinosaur - and a cow, for Felix, once:

"Oct. 31, 1999

Hi LeDon...

We went trick or treating at the zoo today, as a family of devils - with Kasey as our little angel (she reminded me of you). Of course, afterward, we had to go surprise Mom...and she filled their bags with candy, as usual. Of course, Kody and Brian think they're too big now to trick or treat, so this year, it was just the four of us... Kris looked so cute in his little devil costume.

Well, my feet hurt and I'm really tired tonight, so I'm going to lay down - I just wanted to tell you I was thinking of you. I love you. I'll write again soon.

Love always, Denny"

***

Now, after one full year, Brian had a beautiful scar, from his belly button down to his pubic hair - about ½ an inch wide. It healed up amazingly well and faded to almost invisible. Our bodies really are astonishing, you know? Each little 'member' a life all its own... and each one, faithfully doing its part to the keep the 'whole' together and alive.

I think there's a lesson in there somewhere.

"Nov. 30, 1999

Dear LeDon:

We were alone this year for Thanksgiving. Mom and Al went to see Grandma in Utah - and Brian, Kasey and Kody went to South Dakota to spend time with Bob. They don't really like it, but they know it's important to do, sometimes.

Sid, Kris and I went out and had a nice Mexican dinner! We decided to wait until everyone gets back to fix our turkey dinner. It'll be nicer that way.

Well, I'm gonna go now... I promised Kasey we'd get the decorations down today. Later.

Love, Denny"

***

It only seems to take two days for December to go from the first to the twenty-fourth... not quite sure how that works - and the week that follows, is always just a blur. Next thing I know, I'm facing "that day" again:

"Dec. 29, 1999

Dearest Donny...

Four years to the day, almost to the hour... no wonder I haven't been able to sleep yet tonight. It's so hard not to think about - and impossible to forget. The years are beginning to melt into one another, but this day, always stands alone.

Christmas was a little easier this year - Kristofer is more aware of things and he could sense the excitement of the holiday. That seemed to add to the spirit. Since we had our "Thanksgiving" a little bit late, we had Al's Hawaiian teriyaki and egg rolls for Christmas dinner. I had a little extra, for you:-)

Mom played the piano and we sang carols, which we hadn't done since you left us. And though it's not the same without your angelic voice, we did enjoy ourselves for the most part. Mom is finally starting to talk about you again. Not a whole lot, but she is getting better. I guess, time really does ease the pain.

Kasey's birthday is tomorrow. She's nine already! Can you believe that? She reminds more and more of you every day. Well, I better try to get some rest - busy day tomorrow.

Always and forever, I will love you.

Your little sister, Dennel"

***

Chapter 8

I HATE DOCTORS

I had high hopes that 2000 would be a better year... both financially and physically. I was very optimistic, in fact. I felt sure that our "bad luck" was behind us, and I saw this year as an opportunity for rebuilding - but... it doesn't matter how prepared I think I am - life always catches me off-guard:

"Jan. 24, 2000

Hey Donny...

You know, I was working in the front pasture today, when I knelt down and stood back up, to have my right leg muscle (just above the knee) bulge and cramp... guess I was putting too much pressure on that leg because my left knee had been hurting again recently - obviously, neither one is in good shape. It hurt so bad, I cried out in pain, and then looked around to see if anyone was watching me. Luckily, just the horses.

I slowly limped back to the house and called my doctor to see if we could add my right knee to the x-rays already scheduled for tomorrow on my left one!

I'm gonna hobble off to bed now. Tomorrow is going to suck - I hate doctors..."

***

I had the x-rays taken and was scheduled to see the specialist in February. So, once again, I was waiting. I don't like waiting. Even though I dread going to the doctor, it would have been nice to get it over with and get some answers when I really needed them for a change. I get so tired of being told there isn't an answer... and so many times, there are no answers.

But it hurt so bad to walk these days... and with all my other strange aches and pains, coming and going (as they have all of my life), I couldn't help but wonder if it would only continue to get worse over the years. The thought frightened me.

"Feb. 15, 2000

Hey there...

Sorry I never picked back up on my last letter... I've been so terribly frustrated with everything lately - it's hard to even get out of bed. Not just because of my knees, though they do hurt right now, but really, just because. I don't even *want* to get out of bed.

I'm so mad tonight. Had my knee appointment scheduled for this morning - the one to see the specialist. It hurts to walk, it hurts to drive, both knees hurt all the time now.

I picked up Aki, who was going with me to help watch Kris... then went to get my x-rays. The doctor's office was supposed to have them waiting for me, but when I got there, they couldn't find them. I was so upset – mainly, because I was hurting so bad - and I yelled at everyone.

I made a huge scene and demanded that they call to re-schedule my appointment, and tell the specialist it was their fault. They did. But I can't get in to see him until March 2nd now, and Tylenol doesn't even help anymore.

Saw Dr. Todd yesterday (my neck doctor). He was checking to see if the numbness and tingling in my hands is coming from a nerve in my neck.... had an MRI done a week ago, maybe more - I can't remember.

Don't remember much anymore, if I don't write it down.

He said there was nothing he could see on the MRI that

should be causing me any pain - and he sent me on my way.

Typical. He didn't even take the time to feel my neck, or ask me

anything at all.

Hated him more than most. I sure do miss you...

Love Denny"

***

For the next few weeks, I rested as much as possible, and

stayed off my feet as much as I could. I was moving very slowly

these days. At times, it felt like I was literally falling apart.

I remember sitting and thinking one day - when it hurt too

bad to even move - how horrible it would be if this was all I had

left... if I couldn't move a muscle anymore because I was so stiff and

sore... what if I just couldn't get up one day? Somehow, in the back

of my mind, I have always thought that day might actually come... I

certainly hope not.

The thought made me remember LeDon, unable to move,

unable to communicate. I'd have to at least be able to use my hands,

to communicate. I could throw myself into my writing that way -

otherwise, I wouldn't be able to keep my sanity.

Time only seems to go by slowly, when I am in pain. This

year, I could tell, was going to be a long one.

And as if things weren't hectic enough, I was forced to face another huge fear of mine... the dentist. I had to go see the dentist - and I REALLY hate dentists:

"Mar. 6, 2000

Oh, LeDon, how I wish you were here...

I had a really hard day today. Last week, a piece of an old filling broke off my tooth, and - it didn't hurt, but it was sharp on my tongue and was making it sore. So I wanted to see if I could just get it filed down a little bit. I should have just gone back to Dr. Bickston... and paid him cash - I halfway liked him. But no, I tried to find a new dentist that was on our insurance plan and, of course, he wanted to put me through an entire exam... x-rays and everything, before he would even talk to me to see what it was I was there for! And I just couldn't do it.

I freaked out in the dentist chair... hell, you probably saw me - I freaked out before I got to the dentist chair. I don't know why, really, but I was already crying in the waiting room.

I never even saw the dentist - he came in once, but I couldn't look at his face... he had a bad attitude and, immediately, I didn't like him. I tried to tell him I just had a sharp edge I needed to have sanded down, but he wanted to poke all around in there. It was all I could do to stay in that chair for as long as I did just talking to him.

I was very scared and everyone could see that - but no one seemed to care. He certainly didn't care. I shook and cried, and couldn't even bring myself to open my mouth for him.

I finally just told them to forget it... I'd live with it if I had to, and deal with my tongue being raw! Or I'd sand it off myself. I paid them $20 for the visit and I left.

I felt better the minute I walked out that door. I was still shaky and mad, but it didn't take me *too* long to calm down enough to drive. I went home and took a fingernail file to my tooth. It took a while, but got the corner off. Why do I react that way? - I wonder.

All I know is I've always had this intense fear of dentists... Mom told me I hit one once - when I was six years old or so (I've had to get "gassed" ever since). Before I'll even make an appointment with one, I have to know first that they will give me nitrous, and plenty of it... otherwise, I just can't do it. Irrational? Maybe to some - but you know, it's very real for me.

I had my knee appointment on Thursday... but, as usual, the inflammation had subsided somewhat by then, and the doctor couldn't see anything specifically wrong with it. He did tell me that it appeared from my x-rays, that I have little to no muscle around my knees (which I've always known). This is why my knees slide and click - and is probably also the only reason I have pain when twisting or bending.

He gave me knee exercises... a routine, to follow 'like religion' he said – (if he only knew I wasn't good at that). But it seems simple enough. He gave me a prescription for some anti-inflammatories and pain pills. And he said for a week or so, after the exercises, I would probably have to put ice packs on my knees as well. Boy, was he right about those icepacks!

Those exercises are harder than I thought they would be. I only have to lift each leg 6 to 8 inches, holding it for 5 seconds, repeating 5 times... (ha!) I couldn't even get my foot one inch off the ground, holding it almost 3 seconds.

I couldn't believe the lack of strength I had - and it hurt to get that far. I always thought I had rather strong legs. I've certainly used them enough in my life. Guess they're just wearing out.

My knees hurt ten times worse than they ever did before. My legs are all stiff and sore. The pills don't seem to help much.

I've tried resting, but had appointments scheduled for the cable guy, the fridge repair guy - and Kasey had softball practice yesterday. Damn, driving hurts.

Oh, well... I suppose things could be worse. At least I'm in a place where I'm happy. We had a beautiful winter - the sun was shining almost every day by early February - and when it wasn't, it was simply 'fairly cloudy', kind-of-cold and a little bit drizzly. Oh yeah... it's morning now, by the way. I didn't sleep at all last night.

I got potatoes planted by Valentines Day this year... with Kasey's help digging, and within weeks, had my onions, carrots, radishes, cucumbers and corn in the ground.

I love living in the country, you know - you never did understand it when you were here, but maybe you do now. All my animals think they are starving this morning. If I don't make it out there by 9am, they come looking for me - the chickens, ducks and dogs - all sitting by the door, waiting patiently for me to step out. But the second I do, they'll go nuts! They start squawking and quacking, following me back to the barn... and then the guinea pigs start squealing - that gets the horses going - and it makes me smile. They're all so happy to see me in the morning!

All I ever wanted in life is right here, right now. A home, a husband (who's been treating me alright), my children and my animals. At this moment in my life, I am happy... exhausted, but happy. With Kristofer potty training now, and into everything lately, and Kasey in Girl Scouts, basketball and softball - me, being Scout Leader - not to mention doctor's visits, which I still have had a few (and the kids too), this is turning out to be a very busy year for me.

I have a dozen phone calls to make every day, it seems... insurance authorizations, and such - and Girl Scout cookie sales starting April 1st. We still have so much to do before then. Forgive me if I don't find time to write for a while...

I need to go lay down now.

I'll be thinking of you.

Love, Denny"

***

The weeks to follow actually raced along as my knees began to feel better. The exercises were finally helping. I could get my leg a whole 6 inches off the floor now, and almost hold it for the full 5 seconds - and it was a little easier to bend down, and stand back up again - though I had to do it gingerly. But I found that I have to keep up with the exercises - if I go too many days without doing them, my knees start to tell me so.

I continued to do what needed to be done, not realizing that I was pushing myself much too hard. Brian had several appointments too, for his back, which always seemed to hurt him but had been worse since he ran into the sliding glass door that day.

I'm afraid he inherited my weak joints and muscles - he also, has bad knees and wrists... and that break in his hip was not normal. He has always hurt in the strangest of places, since he was little - just as I have endured it all my life - and no one has ever been able to figure out why.

Sooner or later, I hope to get some answers so maybe my kids won't have to suffer like I have... I don't know. But as I sat and fantasized about my life at the moment, and the future I had envisioned... I could never have imagined the reality of what was just around the corner.

***

Chapter 9

IF IT'S NOT ONE THING, IT'S ANOTHER...

Medically, I had already had a pretty rough year, so I decided it was time to start a "medical journal". The whole year ended up being consumed with my deteriorating body and mind... just when I physically started to feel better (stronger and more energetic), I had to start questioning my mental state:

"April 1, 2000

Hi LeDon...

What a day! Kasey's softball tournament, which turned out to be a disaster... a birthday party she "had" to go to, and the cookie booth sale all in the same day. The cookie sales went well - better than I expected - thankfully, I had good help from my girls' moms. And Sid got Kasey to her party ok, but, the tournament... dear Lord, that's another story.

In short, I got in a fight (or rather, a discussion) with the coach, after the first game... because he put Kasey in the outfield for the first inning and sat her on the bench for the rest of the game. He told me that he felt she was too immature to be out there anywhere, and I became very upset. I mean, I literally blew up on the man! Told him things I probably shouldn't have said in front of the kids - but I just couldn't help it. I am so on edge.

I spent all night trying to get a hold of the President, or someone in charge of the softball association, but to no avail... so I finally wrote a 3-page letter to the association, for all the good it will do. I don't expect a response, but it helped me feel better.

Hey... Happy Anniversary :-)"

***

Looking back now, it's hard to even imagine the 'place' I was in... it seems almost insane now. I don't know how, or why, I was trying to do everything that I was doing - or trying to pretend that I was ok the whole time - because I wasn't ok.

My medical journal reveals the truth:

"Sunday, April 2nd... very tired today - had another booth sale to make it through - the other moms ended up sending me home. Took a Tylenol and laid down.

"Monday, April 3rd... I slept the day away today - thank heaven Kristofer was a good boy! He wandered the house (and got into a few minor things) - and kept coming back in the room to check in with me. He could tell I wasn't well... every time I tried to get up and do something, I ended up going back and laying down on the bed again. Hours went by each time and I didn't even realize it until it was evening.

"Tuesday, April 4th... Woke up this morning, feeling refreshed - showered and got ready to go to an appointment I was sure I had with the geneticist this morning... looked in my book to see what time I was supposed to be there, and found my appointment was yesterday - I had missed it! I was so mad! I went back to bed and laid down.

"Wednesday, April 5th... The geneticist thought there might be a link to something called "Stickler Syndrome" in my genes - has to do with joint problems. She said there would be a test for it in a couple more years that could isolate the gene - that would be interesting. I'm still faithfully doing my leg exercises... they really do help. My knees don't hurt much anymore. Now my right wrist hurts - mostly, when I move my thumb the wrong way, or if I rub my hands too hand. My fingers are stiff and swollen most of the time and still going numb at night. The other night, my entire arm suddenly went dead… three times!"

***

I began to feel relief now - because it was 'just my thumb' that was bothering me and not my knees so much anymore. They had hurt for so long. I was relieved to be walking better. It always seemed, that just as one thing would stop hurting me, another would begin... at first just bothersome, then after days or weeks, to the point of painful. Sometimes, one pain became preferable over another (as if I were given a choice).

It was the same, too, with my life... just as one trauma would subside, another would take its place. And so it was to be again:

"Thursday, April 13th ... I cancelled my follow-up with Dr. Daniels (my knee doctor) because I was just too tired to drive to Fort Worth today. Didn't even want to try.

"Friday, April 14th ... Had too many errands to run today - picked up more cookies for tomorrow's both sale... tried to rest.
Not much luck.

"Saturday, April 15th ... I guess everyone could see I was beat. My GS moms offered to take over the booth and let me go home and rest again. I was more than glad to do so.

"Thursday, April 20th ... Busy day - had to do bills (way behind on budgeting). Had a GS pizza party to prepare for (went shopping, cleaned house, etc)... tired tonight!"

***

I was going a mile a minute, it seemed... and I didn't even realize it. I was literally "running on empty" at times, but I had to keep going. There was just so much to do.

Easter was coming, and that was always a special time for us... there was much preparation to be done. Besides, things were actually starting to look up - or so I thought:

"Sat. April 22... Got our tax refund yesterday! Sid needed new tires on his truck so we got new rims too. He took Kris and Kasey, while mom and I did Easter 'stuff' and then I stopped by to pay for the tires. We juggled kids (and 'stuff') and went back to mom's - we painted eggs and videotaped - by days' end, I was exhausted."

***

Easter Sunday was lots of fun, even though I was missing LeDon... after hunting for our baskets, by decoding the bunny clues, and watching Kris wear himself out finding eggs, I crashed. I slept half the day away. Mom woke me up about 4pm to eat and we packed up our baskets and went home.

I had missed a few nights of my leg exercises... (it's hard to remember, when routine changes). But, I was feeling rather optimistic - and getting steadily stronger, it seemed:

"Monday, April 24th ... Bought a new lawn tractor today with the rest of our refund! I couldn't wait to use it... mowed almost the entire lawn (approx. 2 acres) right after it was delivered. It is really fun, and much easier than my push mower."

***

I had fooled myself into thinking I was invincible, I guess.

The signs were all there - yet I paid no attention... I had no energy, but I still wasn't sleeping - I thought I just didn't need that much sleep, since I am an insomniac by nature. For quite some time now, I had let myself slip into a routine of late nights and listless days.

I hadn't even really noticed how exhausted I was... even though I talked about it all the time. I simply lost track of myself somehow... I don't know how, really, it just seems to happen sometimes. Then something strange happened to me- the strangest thing that has ever happened in my life. My body 'yelled' at me.

I actually thought, for the second time ever, that I might die, when I experienced what was probably, one of the scariest moments of my life:

"Tuesday, April 25th ... Spent the day raking up grass and feeding it to the horses, from mowing yesterday - felt pretty strong all day. I've been doing my knee exercises for almost two months now and finally able to do them as the doctor ordered... in fact, tonight, I added 2 seconds holding time to each leg. It was pretty easy, really.

"Approximately 11pm... I felt a sharp, shooting pain in my left arm (which I have felt before)... but then, I became suddenly chilled - and instantly, starting shaking uncontrollably, legs first. I watched my legs for a while, every muscle twitching, as I wondered what was going on. After several minutes, I started to feel severe cramping in my upper thighs. I asked Sid to help me up, to see if I could walk because my legs were getting stiff. I couldn't. He held me in front of him, supporting me, for about ten minutes, as I painfully struggled to get one foot to move in front of the other, and the cramping slowly started to ease. I had him sit me back down on the bed and found I was almost out of breath. I noticed at this time that my hands were beginning to tingle and go numb (which also happens a lot, so I didn't think too much about it)."

***

My legs were still trembling, though not quite as ferociously as before, but still considerably tense, so I leaned back and tried to relax. Sid sat over me and held onto my legs as they quivered - then, I noticed that they, too, were numb. I could barely feel my feet. I laid back, crossed my arms, closed my eyes and took a deep breath - and all of the sudden, EVERYTHING STOPPED. It was so weird. Not a muscle in my body moved, for about 30 seconds. Then I felt "twitch"... "twitch, twitch"... and it started again.

It wasn't as severe as it was at first, but it continued until 11:40pm, and then it finally slowed down and stopped, for good. My heart was racing and my head was throbbing. I took three Tylenol and went to sleep shortly after.

Sid wanted to take me to the E.R. but I kept telling him "no" - I don't know why. I was very scared... but I just didn't want to go. I suppose I should have:

"Wednesday, April 26th ... I woke up feeling as though I had run a marathon. Extremely tired. Muscles sore... otherwise ok (I thought). I got up, helped Kasey dress for school, brushed her hair and found myself short of breath again. I sat on the edge of the bed for a minute, and noticed my upper lip was numb - that scared me. So a little frightened and still very shaky and weak, I told Sid he could now take me to the E.R."

***

On the way there, my arms and hands once again became tingly and started to go numb - and then my right hand started cramping - my fingers curled tightly. It hurt. I was unable to open them... they were completely numb, and totally paralyzed. This was very scary (this had never happened before) and now again, I felt as though I could hardly breath. Sid had to carry me into the emergency room and they began running tests immediately. I was there until 4:30 pm. And of all the tests they did that day, the doctor said the only abnormality was that my 'artery blood' showed an extremely high "bicarbonate" level - and she asked if I had been eating baking soda!?

How silly, I thought - no explanation for anything, but that? But she said whatever the cause of that was, anyway, it wouldn't have initiated a reaction like I had. She sent me home with a diagnosis of "hyperventilation, probably due to anxiety"... and a prescription for Xanax.

Anxiety... WHY NOW? I had certainly been through more stressful times in my life - and I had enjoyed the day, *that* day, in general.

I did get an e-mail from Tanya that day... my brother-in-law's new wife (and my sister's replacement). It was slightly upsetting... but could that have 'been it'? Or did I just "over-do" it, working in the yard? It just didn't make sense. I work hard all the time.

I have over-done it plenty of times before, and nothing like this has ever happened. Nothing even close to this! I have gotten a little bit shaky before, and my hands and fingers do tingle and go numb all the time... but not like this. I have been through things in my life that would have sent others straight into a deep depression... and I have handled it all, with stride.

I am strong - very strong... stronger than most I think. I am strong-willed, and given my size, physically strong. But I was getting older (as we all do)... and I suppose I should have been paying closer attention to my physical AND emotional health.

I realize now, what was wrong. Looking back, it's easy to see - and I have, finally, learned to slow down (though it took me some time). Even after this episode, it took me a while to accept that I couldn't do it all anymore. Sometimes, I still have trouble convincing myself of that fact.

My body had been trying to 'tell' me for quite some time, that it couldn't handle everything I was asking it to do. It was probably a culmination of all the above... I had simply been doing too much, for too long - and had not been caring for myself properly

- and the emotional stress of receiving that letter, I suppose, just might have been enough to trigger the inevitable. I honestly believe it was a 'message' for me... God was telling me to slow down. He does work in mysterious ways, you know.

***

Chapter 10

LEARNING TO SLOW DOWN

I did nothing but sleep for days afterward... and I ended up on one psychiatric medication after another, all summer long and I hated it. I didn't like the way they made me feel so I would complain, and my doctor would try a different one. Either they made my anxiety worse, or made me feel like a zombie all day long.

I was trying to slow down, like I was ordered to... but I didn't want to just sleep my life away! I had too many things that needed to be taken care of - too many things I just loved to do. I guess, I'm a pretty difficult patient:

"Thursday, April 27th ... Saw Dr. Mills today for my 'follow-up' appointment. She wants me to see a neurologist - and gave me a prescription for Zoloft to take daily, but said to still use the Xanax, if I felt another episode coming on. I had to take one about 7pm. It does seem to help.

"Friday, April 28th ... Took my Zoloft, 8am... still shaky, weak and tired - just rested today.

"Saturday, April 29th ... Took Zoloft, 8am... rested - able to stand for slightly longer periods of time - shaky, tired and short of breath.

"Sunday, April 30th ... Took Zoloft, 7am - feeling somewhat better today - still shaky and tired - needed a Xanax at noon. Last cookie sale today.

"Monday, May 1st ... Took Zoloft at 7am - still moving slowly. Did bills, returned cookies... feeling ok. Started leg exercises again tonight – it's hard again now."

***

Once again, circumstance had taken control, and forced me to slow down against my will. I was 'told', in no uncertain terms, to stop trying to do so much - and to start paying more attention to my body. I had to learn to re-prioritize my life... to cut out anything that was not essential, or beneficial to me:

"May 5, 2000

Dear LeDon:

Well, while on doctor's orders to rest, I have more time to write! So I suppose, there is always a positive side to everything. You know I love writing to you... sharing things with you - just makes things seem that much more special. I do feel a little silly, sometimes, though... telling you things, when I know, you've most likely been watching it all anyway. But it makes me feel better somehow, all the same.

So, Little Miss Stormy (my filly) is now almost a yearling. Brian is turning 17 this month, and Kristofer will soon be 2 - and what a handful he is! He is talking so much now! He says please, and thank you... he knows his right from his left, and he can even (almost) dress himself. He can say anything he wants to really, as long as HE wants to. Sissy can get to talk the most - he'll say just about anything for her. He really loves her, you can tell... and you can always see her love for him, in her smile.

He'll repeat the entire ABC's with Kasey, and he can almost count to ten (with help)... he tries to hula-hoop and wishes he could ride a bike... and he loves sitting on the horses. But when I can't take the time to let him do that, he tries sitting on the dogs! They don't care for it so much, but thankfully, they're good with him.

Samantha's sitting on my lap right now - she's been a little distant since Kristofer's arrival. Poor kitty... she's been through all four of my babies with me, and probably felt pushed aside every time. She's been in a lot of pain lately... guess 16 is pretty old for a cat. I have to take her in for cortisone shorts every month or so now.

Well, I better go take my pill! God I hate taking medicine every day - I have trouble even remembering to take vitamins. I love you... talk to you later.

Love Denny"

***

I did, slowly, start feeling better again... and, day by day, had a little more energy - but I really didn't feel like the psych medication was doing anything for me, except making me yawn. I was just tired all the time. I felt like I was walking around in a fog all day... and it was hard to even remember to take it - especially when I didn't feel like it was helping:

"Monday, May 22nd ... Forgot to take my medicine yesterday - all day - we worked on the fence and stayed pretty busy all day, and by the time I remembered that I had forgotten to take it, it was late afternoon, so I went ahead and took it and figured I'll start taking them at night instead.

"Wednesday, May 24th ... Hardly slept at all... I was miserable all night - up and down. Missed Kasey's bus and had to drive her to school. My knees are hurting again... not remembering my exercises. Forgot my medicine yesterday too. Guess I'll try to stick to mornings."

***

I tried hard to follow the doctor's orders, but no matter which medication she put me on - and as the years went by, I went through a bunch of them (Celexa, Paxil, Zoloft) - I had trouble sticking with any of them more than a few months at a time... just didn't feel like they were doing anything for me, except making me tired. None of them made me feel any "better."

At this time, I came to the decision that what I really needed was to make a change in my lifestyle. The whole episode was actually a sort of 'blessing' in disguise. It was really, exactly, what I needed - something to make me focus *on me* - I had simply been doing way too much. I needed to take some 'time-off' in order to get control of my life back.

So by now, I was at least feeling well enough to spend some time with my horses again... and I had finally been given the time.

"May 28, 2000

Oh, I miss you LeDon:

What a nice month it has been. Yesterday was the first truly 'busy' day I've had in a while. Spent all day running errands, buying presents and getting ready for Brian's party today. I tried to get a good night's sleep, but you know how hard it is for me. I felt pretty good all day, considering. I baked Bri's cake, finished wrapping his presents, and Sid cleaned house while I stayed in the kitchen. I am so thankful for Sid right now. If it weren't for him, I would go crazy sometimes I think. Brian had a nice party. I am very tired tonight.

Brian is working at Pappa John's Pizza now. I only see him in passing anymore - it was nice to spend the day with him. Time just seems to fly anymore. Sometimes I can't believe how he has grown - he is so tall now - almost 6 feet. Wasn't it just yesterday that you held him in your arms, so tiny and helpless?

Kody somehow passed me in height too, and I don't know when, exactly. I think I was sleeping. I know he was looking me in the eye at the beginning of the New Year, but now, he is two inches taller! He has matured an awful lot this past year... both physically and emotionally.

Kasey is almost as tall as me now, (of course, I'm only 5'2") - for a girl, not even yet 10, 4'9" is pretty darn tall. She is always such a big help to me... around the house, and with Kris, and the animals. I really don't know what I would do without her.

I almost have my yearling, Stormy, halter broke. She is basically 'gentled" (I can halter her and lead her around, brush her, touch her all over and lift her feet).

I have spent a little time with Dad's 2-year old stallion, Blue, as well. He is a sweetheart. Hope he stays that way.

Guess what? Kasey actually started riding Prince by herself this year! I was quite nervous the first time I turned him loose with her, but she did extremely well controlling him, and he responded amazingly well to her. I really didn't think she'd be ready for him for several more years, so it took me, pleasantly, by surprise. She was so pleased with herself - grinning ear to ear... and I was very proud of her.

You know, I always found spending time with my horses very relaxing - even much more effective than all the medication I've been on. I'm beginning to feel like a walking zombie, being on so many meds.

But I'm learning to focus more on myself, and my family. I am enjoying spending time with them and my animals - and I'm trying not to worry so much about all those 'little things' that were driving me crazy before. I quit doing Girl Scouts, took time off from all sports... and decided to take time to simply 'exist' for a while. It's pretty nice, just "being."

I can only imagine the peace you have. Sometimes, I think, YOU got off easy. Maybe that's the reward for being truly good inside - being released from the burdens of this physical world. But if that's the case, why does your death still seem like a punishment? I'm still so mad at God for taking you away from us - even now, it just doesn't seem fair. I hardly talk to Him anymore.

I keep trying to get in touch with Felix... but he doesn't reply often. I promise I won't even stop trying to reach out to the boys.

They aren't really old enough to stay in touch for themselves, and I understand that... but they soon will be. I will tell them all about you one day. Don't worry about that. They will know you - but if you could do anything from your end, I could use all the help I can get.

I miss you.

Love always... Dennel"

***

Chapter 11

ANOTHER LOSS

This year, would certainly stand out as one that "tested" me to the limit, both physically... and emotionally. With all I was already dealing with, I began to wonder what was going to go wrong next. Then I found out.

I would experience, yet another loss, of someone very dear to me. It was Samantha's turn to go. It was the end of a sixteen-year friendship:

"June 7, 2000

Oh, LeDon...

I found Samantha, laying underneath my Suburban today. I'd been out working in the yard (and earlier, I had noticed her crawl under there), but when I went to call her out from under there to go in the house at the end of the day, she didn't move.

I thought she was looking at me, at first... because her eyes were open - and when I looked closer, I saw that she wasn't breathing. I crawled under to reach her, picked her up and held her... and cried.

She had been there for hours, dead already, I guess - because her mouth and eyes were already dried up. I felt so bad that I hadn't checked on her. I had been working outside pretty much all day and I suppose that's why she was out there.

I felt so neglectful - I should have checked on her sooner - I'm so afraid she may have been suffering - I ought to have been there to comfort her. She was all alone in her very last hours... why didn't I notice what was happening to her?

It was so hard to let go of her. I held her in my arms while Sid dug the hole, and I kissed her and cried, and told her how sorry I was for how she had suffered these past years... (the cancer had progressed and she'd been going downhill for quite sometime).

I am actually glad that it's over for her. She is in so much a better place now. Take care of her for me.

Remember when I rescued her? That little black fuzz ball, with ringworm, sitting in that cage - the way she looked at me with those big golden eyes... there was no way I could leave her there to die. I really believe we were, in some way, soul mates. She drew me there that day... she knew that I had saved her life and she thanked me for it every single day.

She would lay on my chest, purring, for hours, non-stop - endlessly telling me how much she adored me. She would stay there all night, if I didn't move her. For almost fifteen years, we spend our nights that way. She had been with me since Brian was one.

It's still hard to believe that she's really gone. Even though she had been pretty distant since Kristofer's birth... and I was sort of starting to get used to not having her on my chest every night, but I am going to have a hard time not looking for her.

Take care of her for me.

Love, Me..."

***

No more cortisone shots... no more throwing up - no more uncontrollable pottying - and no more miserable days, scratching and biting. Rest in peace, Samantha.

I love you.

"Wednesday, June 7th ... Can't sleep tonight. Not tired at all- well, maybe tired, but wide awake. My mind is racing, my eyes won't close. I can't stop thinking about Samantha. Can't settle my mind down. I really can't tell if this medication is doing anything at all. I still have good days and bad days... still shaky most days. Bad couple of days last week (fingers were twitching so badly, I kept bumping the wrong key)... even had a hard time eating because my spoon was shaking so much, I could barely get it in my mouth!

"Thursday, June 8th ... Didn't sleep a wink, and don't think I could still. It's 8:06 am and I have been writing pretty much all night. Took a break and watched some TV for a while, but just couldn't get to sleep at all."

***

It was actually nice not needing to sleep again. I don't get much opportunity to sit down and write during the day - so I actually get most of my writing done on nights I can't sleep. Yes, there have been many more.

Most nights I do manage to get three or four "good" hours, and now and then I actually manage to fall asleep before midnight and sleep clear through the night, until 7 or so. But I never dared take medication to sleep because, the kids might need something or - I don't know, mostly, just don't like to.

Getting over Samantha took some time - but, eventually, I had to bring myself back to reality and start sleeping "normally" again. I had too many things to do, still. Despite all I had been through, I just had to keep going.

At times, though, my body seemed to barely be functioning. But at this point in my life, I wasn't sure if it was my body I should be most concerned about, or my mind.

***

Chapter 12

WHERE IS MY HEAD AGAIN?

The days seemed to melt into one another, as summer disappeared before my eyes. The only writing I really did during this time, was in my Medical Journal. I had become obsessed with my medical condition - but I had no choice - it overshadowed everything else in my life:

"Saturday, June 10th ... Spent the day cleaning our room - shampooed the mattress and everything - it was starting to drive me crazy. Then, while cooking dinner, my hands 'freaked out' on me - somehow, I lost my grip on a hot pan and burned my arm... then I 'threw' a stick of butter on the floor. My hand just jerked uncontrollably. I sure seem to be twitching a lot more lately and sometimes it really catches me off-guard.

"Sunday, June 11th ... Cleaned the entire rest of the house today (and sprayed for fleas)... vacuumed, mopped, washed (everything but dishes)... the floors were really starting to get to me all over. Forgot

to take my Zoloft until after noon- didn't notice any difference.

"Monday, June 12th ... Had a pretty good day... cleaned up some

wood that had been bothering me - got a portion of my garden

mowed, fixed up Kasey's bike and painted it like new - all while

potty training Kristofer (outside)!"

***

I was feeling more energetic again, and... I suppose, I began

to push myself much too hard, much too fast. So, it's no wonder my

body was reacting like it did - look at all I had done in just three

days. It had only been a little over one month since my so-called

"anxiety attack".

Even though I thought I had understood that I needed to slow

down, I guess I hadn't really given myself the time that I needed

time to recover:

"Wed. June 14th ... It's 1:30 am - (ok, so it's the 15th) - either way,

it's still today to me. I haven't been to sleep yet, so that's what

counts. My twitching was bothering me so bad, I had to get up.

Probably won't be able to type very well - or a whole lot. Might

take a Xanax... sometimes it gets bad enough. I had a pretty good

day - got the rest of the back pasture mowed, picked up dog food for

Aki and turned in recycling with Kasey - but it really doesn't seem

to matter exactly what I do, sometimes, I just get these twitches...

first my finger... then my arm - my foot, my leg - my finger again -

then my head? I'm laying in bed, trying to relax, and I just start

jerking - out of nowhere. I hate it. And I find myself wondering,

"did I do something wrong today?" But there are days I work so

hard in the yard, or in the house, and I don't twitch or hurt at all -

most nights, it's just here and there... now and then... not too

bothersome - (almost unnoticeable to me anymore). At least, I have

come accustomed to it at that level. But tonight it is driving me

crazy! And I'm jumpy, too... my cat just sneezed and I almost

jumped out of my chair... ok - I'm going to take a Xanax now... we'll

see if it helps. My fingers are all swollen and stiff tonight too.

"It's 2:30 am now... still no better - my fingers are jumping all over

the place!

"It's now 3:10 am... I think I am finally feeling better. It's hard to tell sometimes... my fingers are not quite to jumpy tho - might try getting some sleep now."

***

Sounds crazy, I know... I even think it sounds crazy. In fact, it WAS crazy. I still have no idea why that happened so badly those nights - or why it still happens on occasion, but it does. It's really very miserable and quite irritating:

"Thursday, June 15th ... I managed to fall sleep shortly after 3:30 am - woke up at 7, with Kristofer informing me that he "had to pee". Now I'm not sleeping again tonight... it's 12:52am (June 16th) and I had to get up because my jaws were hurting. I guess I've been clenching them again tonight. I never notice myself doing that, until it's too late and already hurts. I also find myself grinding my teeth at times, or just tapping them (in sort of a rhythmic pattern) often spontaneously... and I find it hard to stop once I notice it. That's when I think I am really losing it - honestly, sometimes, I think I am going nuts."

***

Yet, really, I know I am as sane as anyone. But then, that's not saying much. Yes, I am somewhat "obsessive-compulsive' - like that stupid rhythmic tapping of my teeth that I do... and at times, I find myself repeating sentences I have read (on billboards, etc.) - or thoughts I have - and I *have* to repeat it over and over, until it sound's 'just right'... but it never quite does. I'll write more about that in another book.

It's weird, I know. Even stranger... my twitching, sometimes, seems to follow a rhythm. And things have just seemed to worsen over the years... it's all becoming more and more common - sometimes my finger twitch so bad, that I can't type at all - and if I try, it just takes longer to correct all the typos. It is starting to get unbearable at times, and I'm starting to get very scared.

I have to 'stretch my neck every hour or so... because it gets stiff and starts to pinch something (a nerve I guess). If I don't pop it, it cramps up.

I also get this high pitched ringing in my ear - usually one or the other - lasts 30 seconds or so... and then everything goes silent, just briefly... and then slowly starts to come back to normal. Not sure what that's all about –like a radio trying to tune in a frequency.

The twitching is always worse at night, but some days are really hard too. And it seems that just when my knees stop hurting me, my wrist goes out... or I pull my shoulder, or my jaw flares up - or I start getting a lot of headaches (migraines). Sometimes for weeks, day after day, or all the sudden, I am just too tired to do anything at all and I can't figure out why.

Can stress really cause all of that? I guess it can... or at least, make it worse. The strangest part of all my ailments, is how everything comes and goes. But I am grateful for that, because that's the only reason I've been able to put up with it. I know it will eventually quit acting up and go away - until the next time... and somehow knowing that it's temporary always made it more bearable.

As crazy as it seems – it's all very real. This probably happens to a lot more people than will actually admit it - it still happens to me more than I like to admit. But none of it has been as severe as that time.

Looking back now, I realize that I needed this time to "focus" on my body - and to begin to realize the connection between our bodies and our souls. I have learned that when we neglect our bodies, they "talk" to us - and if we don't listen, they will talk louder (until it hurts too badly to ignore). I can only imagine that's because the spirit needs the body, while you we here fulfilling our purpose.

I'm getting better at reading my body language, I think.

"June 30, 2000

Dear LeDon:

Tomorrow is Kirstofer's 2nd birthday. Kody decided that he wanted to have his party tomorrow too - so we are celebrating them together.

I was doing ok... right up until I had to go to Walmart (last minute shopping). There were so many people - I guess, everyone preparing for the 4th of July... I cringed as I walked through the crowded isles. It was all I could do not to turn around and leave.

Driving home, I almost wrecked, when - out of the corner of my eye - I saw a bottle tipping over in the console. Kasey had bought a drink (which wasn't even open yet) and I was so jumpy, I overreacted. I gasped, and grabbed to catch it - I don't even know why. My heart was pounding. Kasey just laughed at me. I took a Xanax as soon as we got home. Join us for the party tomorrow.

Love Denny"

***

The party was fun. Summer was gone before I knew it and we were in for yet another surprise twist. We had been in this home for exactly four years now... and the landlord wasn't going to kick us out as long as we were paying the rent - so we were fairly settled in and planning to stay a while.

I started the process of trying to clean up our credit reports (which wasn't easy, given all we had gone through - especially having let the trailer go back in New Mexico). Mine was about forty pages long. I wrote an eight-page letter of dispute to the first credit bureau and slightly shorter ones to the other two. We had enough negative stuff that was legitimate on there... I had to get the old and incorrect things off, at least!

But, once again... fate had plans for us. It turned out that we would not have the year or so I figured we still needed to get everything prepared - we would soon be in a hurry to move - soon, we would have no choice. It was only a matter of months, before circumstances once again placed me in a no-choice situation, forcing our relocation sooner than we wanted.

One day, while walking through the front pasture, I noticed a small stream, which appeared to be coming from underground - and it had a foul smell to it:

"Sept. 7, 2000

Dear Donny:

Ugh! What next? I called a plumber today, because we have a river of sewage running through our front yard - ok, its just a little trickle, but it just as well be a river. Raw sewage, leaking up from the septic tank leach lines. We were told the lines will have to be replaced. And the landlord isn't going to do it. We've wanted to buy this house all along, but she wouldn't sell - insisting it's worth $200,000 (no way).

Besides the vast number of problems this house has (termites, foundation, insulation, etc.) it's just not worth it. Bummer too, cause I really like the neighborhood. It's going to be hard to find any place else with enough room for us and the animals - that we can afford, with our credit right now. Well, gotta go - lots to do.

Love, Denny"

***

I determined to take control of my life once again and get things back on track - one way or another. We had a lot of important decisions to make now and I wouldn't do it with clouded mind... so I made one more choice (which may not have been a good one):

"September 10th ... I stopped taking all that stupid medication the doctor has had me on all summer. I have had it with doctors again - all any of it did was make me groggy... slowed my thinking... it drained me of all energy - and the summer was gone before I realized it! I decided last week that I wasn't going to take it anymore, and after two days, I feeling more like myself again. I am energized and getting so much more done this week. I feel that I have been awfully neglectful of everything lately... my animals, my kids, my family in general (it's been a long time since I've made a nice dinner, or had any 'routine' at all). It feels good to be back. I put a roast on today!"

***

Of course, dealing with the credit bureaus, loan officers and realtors, was frustrating and extremely exhausting. Still I believed the reward would be well worth it. It was time to stop throwing our money away on renting something that was never going to be ours. Time to buy.

I wrote letters and affidavits... pulled out stuff from six year old files to verify everything and made copies of it all. I got Bob to verify the child support and put it all together. It was a lot of work - and a lot of stress. I tried very hard not to let it get me down... but sometimes, it's unavoidable:

"Monday, September 18th ... Had another one of 'those' days today. I cried most of the day. Every thing just seemed so overwhelming - nothing went right... from the kids' lunch money to the computer - to the house loan to the bills..."

***

There were a lot of times I probably could have taken a Xanax (and many that I probably should have), but didn't. For some reason, I just don't like popping pills at the drop of a pin, in fact - I have to be in pretty bad shape before I realize I need one. Usually, Sid lovingly 'suggests' that I take one, before I think about it.

On top of everything else, as if dealing with our housing problem wasn't enough, I started to have problems with my oldest son, Brian about this time... typical teen stuff really, but it took me by surprise - because he was never a 'typical teen' - this was the first time he'd ever acted this way. He has always been such a good kid... but he seemed to be unusually irresponsible lately. He did have a new girlfriend - and I had to wonder if it had something to do with her. He had 'blown off' work about four times the past couple of weeks, and he skipped first period to go 'visit' her, a time or two - because she wasn't in school. So what else should I think?

The topper came when my mom showed up with a new computer (well, a used one from her work) and it opened up a whole new can of worms.

***

Chapter 13

THE COMPUTER DILEMMA

"Sept. 22, 2000

Oh, My Dear Sister...

How I wish you were here right now... Mom is mad at me again. I can't understand what I did wrong, though. See, she got this 'bigger and better' computer the other day and offered to give it to me for one of the boys – "whoever needed it," she said.

So I told her I would probably give Brian the option first of taking, since he was the oldest, but wasn't sure he'd want to bother having to transfer all of his files and music. However, when I talked to him he said he wanted to - he was just too tired that night to work on it. That was understandable, he had worked that day.

But Saturday, he ended up sleeping the morning away and didn't make it to Saturday School, like he should have (he's failing due to his absences now).

Then he had friends over - without my permission - and partied all afternoon. He blew off work again, and was still 'just hanging' with his friends, at 5pm, when I called him aside and told him how disappointed I was with his behavior that day.

All this time, he had been in his room where he could have been working on disassembling his computer (but chose not to because his friends were there). So, at 8pm, I went to the garage, got the computer and took it into Kody's room. I decided to give it to Kody because he really wanted it. Needless to say, Bri wasn't happy with me... but I had thought long and hard about it before doing it and I was sure I had made the right decision. He was upset, but he handled it well - and I think I got my point across.

Then, for some reason, Mom decided that Brian really should have the computer and she said I should have taken the car keys away instead! But the car had nothing to do with it that day - the issue was the computer, and his laziness. I think I handled the whole thing pretty well.

I remained at all times, able to talk with Brian about the situation - he knew exactly why I did what I did... (this was important to me - that he understood why). He spent a few days sulking about it, and then a few more really thinking about it, and then he came to me yesterday and asked if I would be opposed to him talking to Kody about 'swapping' computers.

I told him he was welcome to talk to him, but I high doubted he would want to, and I wouldn't blame him a bit, and wasn't going to make him go along with it. Brian agreed, but thanked me for giving him the opportunity to ask.

Kody came to me last night and told me that Brian had talked with him about it, and that - to him, it really wasn't that big of a deal. He told Brian he was willing to do it. So they traded computers last night and new everybody is happy again.

Brian learned a very valuable lesson from all this... he accepted his punishment, without throwing a fit, and took the time to diplomatically figure out how to get what he wanted anyway! He realized that he was being pretty thoughtless that day and assured me that he would 'prioritize' a little better in the future when opportunities such as that came his way.

Then, out of the blue, came an email from Aunt Shan (of all people)... lecturing me about how 'mean' I had been to Mom - how I 'barked' at her... (no idea what she's talking about) - Mom and I had a few words over it, but nothing serious!

Her email said: 'Your mom exists for you and your children, and it's very painful to have you be so mean to her. She's entitled to much more than this. She has her opinion and you yours, but she is your Mother. She has plenty of her own worries, and lives paycheck-to-paycheck but always manages to find something for your family. You may need to look inward Denny, and do whatever it takes to help you relieve your stress, get well and be happy. It does no good to yourself or your children, or your husband, to always be tense and unhappy.'

Wow... what's all that about? Was this really coming from our favorite Aunt?? She, of all people should know what Mom is like sometimes - she grew up with us after all! I am going to have to lovingly write her back to tell her that I don't need to be chewed out by her when she doesn't even have all the facts.

Mom gave me that computer and told me to do with it as I wished... so I did - then she tried to make me undo what I had done, when she decided Brian should have it, regardless of how he was acting. I'm not sorry... I'm a good mother and I have always had a great relationship with my kids. I don't need to be told how to handle them by anybody. I also don't need to be told how to treat my mother - I hadn't even been mean to her! I love Mom. Always

have and always will, no matter what.

Sometimes, we may not agree on certain issues - but that is a

mute point when it comes to my love for her... and I know she feels

the same way. She just has a hard time showing it. I believe that I

have always treated her with all the respect she deserves , whether

we are arguing or not - and always, with love.

So just what did Mom say to her, I wonder, to make her think

I was being mean? And I'm not carrying any 'burdens' from your

death, like she implied - at least, not that I don't realize - and what

does that have to do with the whole computer issue anyway?!

I had a lousy day on Monday... that's all. My, being in tears

most of the day, had nothing whatsoever to do with you... I miss you

every day - and I have lots of good days in spite of it.

So, I sent an email to Mom, letter her know that I didn't

understand what I had done that was so mean to her. I told her I

respected her opinion. That's why I called to let her know what I

had with the computer... but I didn't believe, just because I 'owe' her

for raising me and always being there, that she had the right to tell

me how to discipline or reward my children.

I told her, I realize, always, how much she does for us - but I was under the assumption that she did it because she loved us and wanted to... not so that I would 'owe' her. It's not like I'm always asking for her help - most of the time, what she does for us, she does on her own - usually without my prior knowledge (as with this computer).

Believe me, I have looked 'inward' more this year, than ever before in my life! My stress is not in there. I am, and always have been, a generally happy person - in fact, most of the time, people wonder why I am so happy and optimistic. You know I am not 'always tense and unhappy', as Shannon insinuated. I love our aunt, but she was really out of line here.

I also told Mom that I didn't think I was being sensitive, angry and critical (like she thought) over the computer. I believe I was using common sense and not a hot head, when I made the decision I made - and it all worked out fine!

Then, I added... 'I don't know about you Mom (because every time I bring up LeDon, you won't talk about her) but I am not 'psyched out' about her death.

No - nothing about her death made sense, and it never will -

but I have not allowed it to drive me crazy. As hard as it was on me, Mom - I know it had to be even harder on you. I couldn't imagine losing one of my children, no matter how old they were. I am sure it is devastating... but you really should have allowed yourself to fall apart sooner! You could accept it, if you truly believed that our spirits never really die.

LeDon didn't really leave us. Her spirit just moved on - call it Heaven, the other side, or whatever you want... but there is a place where we go - I am sure of that even if you aren't. And when we go there, we have the ability to watch over those we love and help guide them. I believe LeDon does that for us now. This is my peace of mind... I truly hope, one day, you can find yours.'

I ended it with, 'I would be happy to talk to you more about this, if you want to. I, too, am always here for you - if you need me.'

I think about everything, all the time, Donny - about you, about how senseless your death was... whether there was any 'reason' or 'purpose' that God would have needed you more than those boys do. And although, I find that hard to believe, I have come to understand a little bit better this year, that perhaps, on a spiritual level, it was actually your choice to leave.

If Mom is on the verge of a nervous breakdown (almost five years after the fact), it is because she hasn't allowed herself to deal with your death yet. For all these years, anytime I mention your name, she would change the subject or cut me short... as if she's pretending that you still live in Vegas and just never call. Her face would instantly change expression - and she will only speak of the boys a sentence at a time. I wish I knew how to get through to her. Why is it that Mom and I can never see eye to eye on anything? Something as simple as a dispute over a stupid computer can blow up into the deepest discussion!

I sent the email and hoped for the best. Help me, if you can.

All my love, Denny"

***

Chapter 14

FATE AT WORK

The day after I sent the email, I received one back from my mom that said: "was your email supposed to be blank? Perhaps it is for the best"... Sometimes fate is a scary thing – because, some how, it just always seems to know what is right.

My computer said everything worked normally when I sent it... I honestly don't know what happened. No - it was not supposed to be blank! I had put a lot of work into that letter and I wanted her to hear all those things. But I wasn't a bit surprised when I pulled up my horoscope that day, and it said:

"Leo, bite your tongue - think carefully about what you want to say - time will make everything sound better..."

I knew right then, fate was at work... Someone reached out and snatched that email as I was sending it! I tried to retrieve it from my sent box, but it was just gone! My folders had all disappeared from my Juno files and I couldn't find it anywhere.

If it wasn't the hand of 'fate' at work here, then it must have been the guidance of my sister. Perhaps, it was for the best, as Mom had said - at least, for the time being. Mom probably wasn't ready to hear all of that yet.

It was just as well. We had another trauma to deal with at this time:

"Nov. 3, 2000

Dear LeDon:

We spent all night Monday night in the emergency room with Kristofer. We were actually on our way there with Kasey - because of a spider bite, when Kris started throwing up severely. He threw up eight times after we got there too, so we asked to have him looked at.

Well, by the time they got us into a room, they said he was 'one sick little boy'... he was extremely dehydrated and could have died. They put him IVs for four hours!

I dread to think what would have happened to him if we hadn't already been en route to the hospital - thank God for that spider! Kasey was fine.

I finally wrote back to Shannon. It took me some time to respond, because I didn't want to say anything the wrong way.

She always felt more like a sister to me than an aunt, and even though I didn't feel it was her place to say the things she said, I certainly understood her desire to 'stand up' for her sister. So I tried to keep it as sweet as possible, because I knew she meant well - and I love her too.

I chose to write her an actual letter, rather than an email, because it just felt more appropriate - and because, I just really miss sitting down and writing sometimes.

I filled her in on the 'discussion' Mom and I had over the computer - and how, somewhere in that discussion, I had told her that Kristofer had broken my nose a few nights earlier... (by slamming his head back into my face). I guess that's why Mom thought I was 'snarling'.

After having talked it over with her (which we are always able to do), she told me that she just couldn't believe I wouldn't go to the doctor for it... and that was what worried her.

But I simply felt the doctor wouldn't be able to do anything more for it than I did on my own. It was up high, right between my eyes - so I made a sturdy little splint out of a Q-tip and taped it best I could. It was extremely sore for about two days and then started healing, and now it is fine.

I also told her that I realized she was only getting a portion of what we really going on here - only hearing what Mom wants her to hear - but asked her to please believe me when I say I *am* happy. Right now, I am happier than I have ever been. I've been doing lots of writing this year... and that, too, makes me happy.

You know, I've even played with the idea of writing some children's books... and talked with Mom about illustrating them for me. Of course, she is always so negative when I come up with a new idea... she thinks I am only dreaming. But she will think differently when my first book is published.

I acknowledged the fact that, for the time being at least (especially because we are trying to buy a house), things are pretty tight financially... and a few bills are falling behind. But I have no doubt that things will only continue to get better. Since moving here, Sid has obtained his Wireman's License and is studying for his Journeyman's.

His former boss called him back because they missed him so

much, and his is making more money than he has ever made in his life... and his salary is bound to continue to increase. This area is growing like crazy and there is so much work for him to be found - and I know God will not abandon us.

As far as the medication goes... I told her I quit taking that last month and feel better now than I had all summer. Honestly, sometimes I get better results from just taking it easy, thinking, praying and writing. I am thinking clearer now than I have been able to think in a very long time - and I'm not burying anything inside.

I told her Mom is the one who has done that. Told her I've tried time and time again to talk with Mom about your death - and she won't talk about it.

I assured her that Mom had taught me to be strong enough to stand up for what I believed... and that's all I was doing when I made that decision about the computer - and as far as my nose was concerned, I simply didn't see the sense in acquiring any more medical bills. Promised her that I didn't mean to offend anyone with my words - and I hoped she didn't take anything the wrong way - but I believe in being open and honest.

It's just the way I am. I hate lying and don't like it when

people hide their true feelings. This world would be so much a better place if everyone would just be open and truthful about the way they feel about things.

I told her that I am finally at peace with your death. It is the way it is, and there is nothing we can do to change it - and I told her that I honestly feel you are closer to me now than you ever were in life. I mean, when your spirit was with your physical body, we were always at a distance and that distance is no longer there.

I explained how special she has always been to me - that of all my aunts, we have been the closest and I have always admired her; that I hoped she didn't think any less of me because I chose to live my life my way rather than how mom wanted me to live it.

I have always just tired to be a 'good' person, to help others when I can and to take care of the things that God has given me.

I also asked her not to think any less of me because I didn't believe God required us to sit in a church to praise him... or to pray out loud to be heard by him... or to 'belong' to an organized religion in order to be accepted by him.

I explained to her how I never felt closer to God than when I was on my horse, sitting high on a mountaintop - listening to the birds, and the crickets, and the breeze blowing through the leaves on the trees that surrounded me. That is where I most easily connected with Him.

I welcomed her to write me back, but I haven't heard anything from her yet. Maybe she's just been too busy.

I don't know. I'm kind of jealous that she got to spend so much time with you that last summer of your life, but I am glad for her, that you two had that time together. I wish we could have had a little more time together, you and I. I sure do miss you - the years rolling by don't change that.

You know, I am really worried about the boys now... even at a loss about what to do. The last time I heard from Felix, he informed me that he had become an Atheist and does not allow the boys to celebrate Christmas or Easter, or Halloween, anymore.

I find that extremely sad because those things were always so special to you.

I don't worry that they are being taken care of materially - Felix always was a good father. They will not lack for anything that way, I am sure... just the traditions that he has now taken away from them. But I know you will be watching over them as they grow, and someday, they too, will realize that you are there.

They will find their way - in spite of Felix - and in the meantime, I will not stop trying to get back in touch with them.

Always and forever...

Your little sister, Dennel"

***

Chapter 15

HANG ON... THE RIDE'S NOT OVER YET

It's amazing what stuff comes back to haunt you from years past, when you try to buy a house! All those things I thought I had gotten over long ago - taken care of and put behind me - ha! They came back at me with a vengeance. I had figured our 'good' credit, which we had been establishing for the past two or three (almost four) years would override all the problems we had five and six years ago... but, boy was I wrong.

Ever since we moved here to Texas, things have been steadily getting better - our credit report does show this. Sid's income has increased every year. I have been able to get the bills slowly back on track... sometimes, even a little ahead.

This past year, in particular, we had received all kinds of credit offers and credit cards we didn't even apply for - so I figured it wouldn't be that hard to get someone to consider us as potential home buyers.

Once I finally convinced someone that we were worthy of

their credit, we were told that they would only loan us $105,000,

even though we had pre-qualified for $130,000. We were

considered a high credit risk.

The next task was finding a house, in that price range, that

'suited' our needs and our lender... they refused to loan on a mobile

home - so that exhausted over half our possibilities. There were

several nice trailers I had already found, with plenty of land... and I

would have moved into any one of them in a heartbeat. But now, it

had to be an actual stick-framed house - and that made it harder with

only $105,000 loan approval.

We had our eye on a beautiful place in Alvarado (about 20

miles South of us), on five acres... a nice country-style home (a

beautiful 2 story), huge workshop, huge dog run, separate pastures,

long driveway - and fruit trees... it was wonderful! It would have

worked perfectly for us - and it was even within our price range -

actually, lower. But we were hesitant, since it was the first thing we

had found, and we didn't want to make a hasty decision, so we

decided to keep looking for a while. We should have known better.

One week later, we regretted that decision. We called to tell

them we wanted to make on offer on the house after all, and it had already sold. After that, we ended up having great difficulty finding another home that price.

There was one of East Broad... on three acres, a little bit closer to Mom's - it was rather small, but unique - and we could have made it work, but they wanted too much for that one. Then there was one way out on West Broad, on only two acres, but it was a huge 2 story - and even though it had a pending contract on it, they didn't want that much, so we thought that we could make it work. But it ended up having foundation problems in the kitchen and we ended up having too little time to deal with it.

While we were still trying to find a house to move into, we began to have even more problems with the rental we were in.

"Nov. 14, 2000

Dear LeDon:

Boy... What a month it has been! I swear, sometimes, when I think things just couldn't possibly get worse, they do. It seems I am always facing one crises or another. They say bad things happen in threes. Well, I tend to get them in sixes, or nines.

As if it weren't bad enough, that every spring we have to endure the swarms of termites that come out of the walls of this house, last week, the toilet overflowed again. Normally, just letting it set for a few hours would alleviate the problem, but this day, it would not. So I called our landlord - she told me to go ahead and call a plumber again.

This time, the plumber informed us that our problem is two-fold. Beside the leach lines which are leaking and need replacing in the yard, the pipes which are running from the house to the septic tank, run downhill, toward the house... so whenever the septic is backed up (due to the saturated leach lines) the water flows back into the house pipes and out of the toilet.

He also told us that the sewer pipes underneath the house are cracked. Lovely, huh? He says, there is nothing they can do about it, without replacing the entire septic system - and there is no way Jo is going to do that! So I sure hope we can find another house soon."

***

But it wasn't to be soon enough... I mean, I started looking – and I found I really nice house, on five acres, a 4 bedroom 2 bath, two-story house with a wrap-around porch on both stories. The master bedroom on the upstairs overlooked the front. A little back yard, and two separate pastures, front and side; it had a two story garage as well, which would have been awesome for both Brian and my dad, and it was only $95,000.00. The land was already fenced, and subdivided for horses; there was even a big dog run and walk-in rabbit pen on the property. It also had huge oak trees lining two sides of the back of the land and several fruit trees growing out front; it seemed perfect.

I took it as a sign that it was meant to be mine, when I walked into the little kitchen and saw jars of homemade jelly sitting in the window, which looked out into the back yard. It seemed to be ideal in almost every way; but the one thing Sid didn't like about it was that the ceiling on the first floor was rather low (they had dropped it with some decorative tiles, which probably could have been removed easily). But it was the first house we had looked at, and we talked about having made mistakes before by jumping on the first thing we saw, so we thought we'd take a few days and see what else was out there.

When I called the realtor back five days later to tell her we wanted it, she said there was already another offer on it. Figures.

Then early one evening, we were nearly asphyxiated! It had been raining, endlessly, for weeks - and that made the plumbing problems worse than normal.

As I was standing in the kitchen that night, cooking dinner, I began to smell 'gas' coming from the heater vent. But this house was all electric! So I called Sid from the room and asked him to humor me a moment... 'tell me why I smell gas coming from our electric furnace,' I said – and he was as dumbfounded as I was. So, of course, I called Mom, to ask her advice. She told me to call the fire department.

When the firemen came, they told us the methane gas fumes were coming from the cracked pipes underneath the bathroom. The sewage from the backed up septic tank was leaking through and flowing into the crawl space. It started coming up out of the vents when we kicked the heater on. The reading on their meter, they said, was at a very dangerous level.

"Nov 19, 2000

Ugh... Hey LeDon:

Well, we had to leave the house for good. Circumstances will allow us no more time there - we were literally forced out by methane gas fumes today! The leach line had backed up and was flowing out of a cracked pipe underneath the crawl space; the fumes were getting sucked up by the furnace, heated up and forced out the vents. Gross, huh? I find it odd that our very own waste can become toxic to us. Can you believe something like this is happening now? What else can possibly go wrong?

The firemen came and checked the vents with their little meter... and it went nuts, it squealed and registered 'at a dangerous level'. That's all they would tell us. They suggested we leave as soon as possible and spend as little time there as we can, while packing during the day. They said we should definitely not sleep there - and not to come back more than absolutely necessary. That is going to be difficult to do because we are not even nearly done packing. We weren't anywhere close to ready, since we haven't even found a house yet. Nonetheless, we packed ourselves up and headed to Mom's.

We are sleeping here for the time being, and going back to finish packing during the day. Happy Thanksgiving, huh? I'm going to bed.

I Love You, Denny"

***

In addition to everything else, the next day, I was contacted by a code enforcement officer from the City of Mansfield, who informed me that the house was going to have to be condemned.

After I explained our situation, he agreed to withhold the condemnation proceedings until the first of December, to allow us a little more time to get completely out of the house.

I still had to find some place to put all my animals... of course, the cats and dogs would be welcome at Mom's with us, but there was just no room for the rest of the kritters. Luckily, my kids' former bus driver offered to put up all of them, if necessary. And I was so grateful for her offer, as the events unfolded in the following weeks.

I tried my best to keep the kids in school, too, but it became increasingly difficult. Kody was the first one I took out, so he could help me pull down all the fencing. We moved my horses all to the back and tore down the front pasture fence, gate and posts first... and took apart my garden next - then the play yard - everything that made it 'home'. Everything that we had put in, we took out.

We packed as much as we could inside, while taking frequent

breaks to go outside for fresh air... (the fumes weren't too bad during the day, as long as the doors were left open) - still, each night I would go back to Mom's and cough and choke for hours. My throat was sore for a week afterward too. Once the rain ceased, and things started drying out again, the fumes weren't so bad and we were able to spend more time packing inside.

During all of this, I did manage to find another house that seemed to be workable - and it was exactly $105,000 (on 2.66 acres). It was only 3 bedrooms (1,000 sq. ft.) but had a double garage, two storage sheds and a pool. It was 16 miles further out, and small, but financially, it would work for us, if we turned the garage into a room for Brian. Sid and I would sleep in the living room until we could do that, but it seemed to be our best option at this point. We got the horses, and chickens - and rabbits and guinea pigs, all moved to the bus driver's property. We put up temporary fencing, threw up pens and used sheds that were there, and went back daily to take care of everybody.

Everything else was out of our hands now. The following week, was just 'wait and see'.

***

Chapter 16

IT JUST WASN'T MEANT TO BE

Unfortunately, when we received the 'title commitment' papers, there were Covenants and Restrictions galore - the realtor had flat out lied to me. According to these restrictions, I would only be able to have two of my horses on the entire lot - and none of the chickens…other animals were limited.

I spent two solid days in tears, trying to figure out what to do. We were supposed to close in six days. Mom and I brain-stormed and typed up a beautiful set of Amended Covenants, which basically just brought everyone already living in the neighborhood into compliance - and we told the realtor she had to get a majority of the lot owners to sign them or we wanted our earnest money back. This, of course, was over Thanksgiving weekend.

Thanksgiving was a little bit difficult. I think things were tense anyway, with us 'living' there - Mom and Al were used to being alone - and I had invited Aki (my Japanese lady-friend) to spend it with us, several weeks earlier, knowing that my mother really wouldn't mind. Aki's husband had divorced her the prior year, after 32 years of marriage - she had no other family and Mom was always the kind of person to take in those who had no where else to go. Much to my surprise, Mom made it difficult on me this time. Granted, I forgot to let her know, until just the day before - but when I asked, "you don't mind that I invited Aki to come, do you?"

I was taken back by her reaction. She became very offensive and told me that I had no right inviting anyone to 'her' house without asking her first... (so, I figured I just as well go ahead and tell her that Sid's brother had called the night before, saying he and his girlfriend had no place to go either, so he had invited them out, as well). She was furious. She insisted that I go ask Al's permission to have everyone come over. Al (my step-dad), who, just days before had fought with Mom over a steak - because he was mad that she allowed my son to eat it! He even called Kody a 'pig,' and said he didn't think steak needed to be "wasted on children."

That night, Mom had explained to me that Al was deprived as a child - he was raised in a poor Hawaiian home. They had very little food and so food was the most important thing in the world to him. I sort of understood - but it didn't explain *her* reaction.

Curiously enough, we had been discussing this in previous days, a story that her grandmother used to tell... the legend of the woodpecker - I liked it very much - and it goes like this:

"Once, when St. Peter was down walking around the earth, as he often did... he came upon the cottage of an old woman, baking pies. He asked the woman, for just one pie, as he had been fasting for days and was very hungry. The woman looked at all her pies, and thought that they were much too large to give away, so she took a small piece of dough, and baked it, but alas it seemed as big as the others when it was done. She thought to herself that all of her pies were much too wonderful to share - so she told St. Peter that she had none to give. St. Peter told her that she was much too stingy to live in human form, and he changed her into a woodpecker - she flew up the chimney (wearing her red bonnet, which remained the same), and her clothing singed to gray... she forges for her food to this day, by endlessly pecking wood."

***

The moral of this story, of course, is not to think that what you have is too great to share, but that what you share makes what you have, even greater.

We did have a wonderful dinner - it was elegant, as I knew it would be. My mother is always a most gracious host. I offered the prayer, which was very meaningful to me.

I thanked God for giving me such a wonderful role model, in my mother - and for teaching me that no matter how little you have, there is always plenty to share. It is because of her, that I am the way I am. She has been both, an extremely positive influence in my life, and - at certain times, a negative one - but, I have always learned from her example, no matter what. She has taught me both what to do, and sometimes, what not to do. She is, deep down, a very giving, loving person - but she can also be, at times, extremely cruel. She has been that way all of my life... I love her, in spite of it.

The realtor called the next day to say she had 26 signatures, out of 30, so it appeared that I could keep all the animals... but, as I have learned time and time again, things are not always as they appear:

"Dec. 19, 2000

Hey Donny...

So it looked like we were going to be closing on that house by December 1st after all - and then, the lender said 'wait a minute' - something was wrong with the appraisal. For some reason, someone had put on the original appraisal that the house was a manufactured home... even though it wasn't. So the lender wanted to get their own appraisal on it before we could close. His appraiser came back, after four agonizing days, and said the house was only worth $80,000! So they wouldn't make the loan on it. I guess it just wasn't meant to be.

So I've resigned myself to the fact that we were going to be stuck at Mom's for a while, and began cleaning out closets to make room for our stuff. After all, I figured, even if I found another house right away, no one was going to want to move right before the holidays. But I decided to make just a few more phone calls, from some old clippings in my purse - other 'remote possibilities' I had been holding onto.

I just happened to get a hold of a lady, who had just happened to show a house that very morning to someone else, near Mansfield, on almost 3 acres, for $95,000.00; which, conveniently, just happened to be vacant!

I immediately asked her to show it to me. I had a good feeling about it and had to see it - I met her at the house two hours later, and signed the offer papers on sight. The minute I stepped onto the property, I told Kody 'I feel at home'. I showed it to Sid that night and he seemed to happy with it. It's only minutes away from his work and does have everything we need. Just enough room for all of us, and our stuff... it felt right. It seemed perfect... and everything rolled smoothly on this house - like it was 'meant to be'.

It took just two weeks to get the paperwork finalized. We closed today and we're moving in tomorrow... four days before Christmas. God, is it really only four days 'till Christmas?

You know, I always try to tell myself, when something is meant to be it will be easy... but sometimes, I forget that too. I should have known from all the hell we went through on the other place, it wasn't meant to be. I keep thinking that we should have taken that very first house that we looked at. I'm pretty sure it's because we didn't, that we went through all this. I feel like God offered us that first house, with every single thing we needed... (the mortgage company would have loved it as it was well worth it) - and we just turned our noses at it, to "see what else was out there."

Look what that got us... three months of hell, and now, just the bare necessities. This house has 'just enough' of everything we need. Things just barely fit in all the cupboards. There is barely enough room for our furniture and things. It has exactly half the land the other one had - it feels like both a blessing AND a punishment. A constant reminder that we could have had so much more, if only we had accepted what was being presented to us at the time.

It's just that we had gotten ourselves into trouble before by making hasty decisions - like the move from South Dakota to New Mexico. But then again... it got us here. And we can't live in the past. Should have, would have, could have... there's a lot of those - but right now, we only have the present.

We learn from our mistakes (hopefully) and we move on. That's the point of life, I think. I'm sure we are still right where we're supposed to be, in order to meet whomever we are bound to meet, and do what ever He wants us to do.

Once again, I feel as if things will be ok. Someone is smiling down upon me from above. Three steps forward, two steps back - time to move forward again. Well... I better get some sleep now - tomorrow is going to be another busy day. I love you.

Always, Denny"

***

Sometimes, there are just certain obstacles we must overcome in order to achieve what we want - so we have to keep trying, when we really want something. But we have to accept, too, that sometimes, if we don't see when an opportunity is being presented to us for our benefit, that opportunity will be taken away.

I knew that first house was perfect for us. It was more than perfect... it was like a dream. And now it is - just a dream.

I won't be making there though; I'll miss that. There are no fruit trees on this property whatsoever. I'll have to start from scratch again. That's my punishment. I am settling once again... and starting over because I didn't see the gift that was in front of me.

***

Chapter 17

SOMETIMES

Sometimes I think, no matter how hard I try, I just can't do anything right. I always think, and I think and think... and I make plans... but things just never seem to go like I plan. I try so hard to look forward - to think things through - all possibilities. I carefully put together a plan of action... getting prepared for whatever may come (ha ha), as if that's possible.

Just when I think I have everything pretty well under control, something happens to throw me off course - to remind me that I am not the one in control - and I have to change my plans.

I always do everything I possibly can to 'cover all the bases'... but something unexpected is always thrown into the works... something totally, completely, unexpected - always. But I have come to determine that there is an explanation for this. God likes to challenge us.

He doesn't like to make it easy. Why, where would the lesson be in that, if we had no challenges in life - if it were easy? He leads us down certain paths... each of ours different - but to the same end. We, of course, have no true idea what that end is.

Living by faith (or blindly, with no faith at all), we struggle to get through each day.

But there is a reason for everything. I have always believed that and have never been given a reason to believe otherwise - because every time things don't go my way, I end up learning a lesson. I see, "oh, that's what that was for"... because I am forced to open my eyes at that moment, to use my head, and search my soul in order to overcome the obstacle.

Yeah, sometimes, no matter how hard you try, things just don't go like you plan... they're not supposed to. There is always something new to deal with in life - that's how we learn.

So just when you think you have it under control, knowing right where you are headed, don't be surprised when fate jumps out and says: "Oh, no you don't - figure this one out!"

This whole 'house' ordeal, was nothing more than another test of my faith. Everything that could possibly go wrong, did go wrong - because we turned down that first opportunity that was being, literally, 'handed to us' by God. But since I continued to ask

Him for help... and never truly gave up hope - and kept trying, making that last phone call that led us here, He was still faithful and provided another opportunity. He gave us just what we needed.

I knew, no matter what happened, it would still turn out for the best. He is always there for me that way. So, even though, sometimes it really does seem like the whole world is against you and nothing else can possibly go wrong - until it does - just try to stick it out. Remember, everything does eventually get better. "This too, shall pass", as my mother always used to say.

You just have to get through each day... fate rarely gives you more than you can handle (although, sometimes, it feels very close). Even though sometimes, you find yourself wondering if it is ever going to end... (believe me, I've been there) - you shouldn't give up. I don't give up, ever. I will fight till there is no more fight in me.

Through this whole ordeal, I kept my spirits high, even when I felt low. I knew God would not let me down in the end... I knew He would find us something else.

I told everyone that I knew I would find a place eventually - and then it happened even faster than I expected. All my life, I've said: You can only go downhill for so long, before you hit bottom, and you have to start going back up again!

I like to think of life that way - as a rollercoaster ride - at least, that's the way mine has been. And the key, I think, to a successful ride, is learning how to cope with the bumps... learning to handle all the downhill slides (no matter how long, or close together) and learning to enjoy the uphill rides while they last - not taking anything for granted, as I did from time to time.

Most importantly, we have to learn to most the most of the entire ride, whether going uphill or down. There are lessons to be learned around every corner - some easy, some not so... but all very valuable, no matter how big or small.

Every event in our life leads us to the next one... and in order to enjoy life to the fullest, we must learn to make the wisest choices possible, as each opportunity is presented. Turning down that beautiful house was not a wise choice on our part, and that opportunity was quickly taken away.

So, given the circumstances, we must be willing to move on each time fate closes another door.

Most of all, we need to remember, so we can learn from our mistakes, as well as from our achievements - and to use all of these lessons to our benefit in the future.

I don't mean to preach here - by all means, I'm not perfect. I still have "those days"... the ones that are really hard to get through... when every little thing goes wrong (and the headache just won't go away). You know, those days when the whole family seems to be getting on each other's nerves, and you find yourself yelling more often than not - those are the days you just want to take a pill or something:

"Jan 5, 2001

My Dear Sister:

It's your birthday today... Happy Birthday.

Kasey came into my room tonight, after a yelling episode in the living room, between Kody and Sid (with me in the middle), over the garbage and Kody's un-wiped, bare feet, which had gotten muddy on the way out to the burn barrel... which culminated into Sid yelling at Kody to wipe his feet before tracking mud onto the carpet, Kody yelling that there was no where for him to wipe them, and me yelling at both of them to stop (all the while, trying to calmly tell Kody that he really should have thought to slip shoes on before taking the garbage out in the mud, so he could have taken them off before coming back in) and all the while, feeling guilty myself because I really should have purchased that 'welcome mat', that I mentally struggled over for ten minutes in Walmart (and almost put in my cart) just the other day.

At the time, it was hard to determine if it should be a priority - and now, tonight, I thought - I would have gladly paid twice the price to have had it here.

Kasey stood beside me, as I sat there on my bed (trying to re-think what had just happened)... and she asked me, as she patted my leg "Mom, did you take one of your pills, so you'll feel better?"

I found myself almost snapping at her, "No - I'm not going to take a Xanax every time everybody starts yelling!" And then I felt horrible about it.

How sad that a child should think that the solution to a 'bad day' is taking a pill - and then, I thought, 'maybe I should take one'? But I didn't - because I hate to. Why can't everyone just get along!? I hate feeling tense and angry, but why should I have to pop a pill just because every one else wants to yell? All I want is a little peace.

And then there are the bills. You know, the ones that just keep piling up all over the desk (although, be it in somewhat-

organized piles).   Sometimes I feel so lost - sometimes, it's just hard
to think. Dear God, please help me make it through this one!

Yes... some days are really hard to make it through...
especially, without you. Christmas without you is just not the same.
You were our 'game planner', our 'director' and our 'entertainer' -
you loved running things on Christmas Eve and we all miss that.

But for the first time, since your death, Mom seemed to be
almost back to herself again. She was full of Christmas spirit and
ready to play games and sing... we played charades and trivial
pursuit - it was nice, to see her smiling again. She can actually talk
about you, a little, without crying now. Although, it is still hard for
all of us - it does get easier, year by year.

Eventually, the realization hits - life goes on, with or without
you. And those of us left here have no choice but to catch up with it
sooner or later, like it or not.

Happy Birthday, LeDon...

I love you, Deny"

***

Chapter 18

OUR GUARDIAN ANGEL

It was hard to believe it had been five years already. Donny would have been 38 now - I, was 36... how quickly the years do pass. Having just moved into our new home, days before Christmas, things were a mess when we came back from Mom's Christmas Day. There were boxes everywhere - so much, still, to unpack.

We did a little remodeling right away - closed in the back porch and extended the dining room and kitchen area. It was messy, but then, everything was already a mess so it made sense to get it all done at once... but it was nice to finally get things cleaned up and put away.

"January 8, 2001

Hey Sis...

Got two of my horses moved out here last night, just finished the fence the other day... trying to finish the chicken coop now so I can get everybody home. It has been hard not having all my animals around me.

But we have been working hard, and staying very busy, putting the house together... Mom and Al have helped a lot - building shelves and repairing things. They made me some lovely shelves above my desk here, spanning two walls, where I am going to put my stuffed animal collection, as well as shelves in our master closet - and taught Sid how to do it; then he did the hall closet and both boys' rooms.

They also built an entire cabinet, which holds our microwave and shelves extending the kitchen wall into the dinning room, oh yeah, and built me a new table, with benches. Mom tore down a wall here, put up a wall there, and *what a difference* it makes! Dad is working now on building his room in the garage.

I still have a lot of organizing to do, plus painting, staining, etc., you know, finishing everything Mom started... but mainly, I want to get all my babies home again. It's so nice to see Missy and Blue out there in the pasture. I hope Prince isn't a shit this time about getting in the trailer... he cut himself up last time!

I'm gonna lay down now. A lot still to do tomorrow - gotta try to sleep tonight.

I love you... Denny"

***

"January 21, 2001

Sid and I were drawing and discussing 'plans for expansion' tonight... how nice it is to be able to think of a permanent future some place at last! I have gotten quite a few more boxes unpacked (finding a lot of 'missing' stuff). My teddy bear shelves are getting full - (it's nice to get my whole collection back together again) - some of them, I haven't seen in years!

It's wonderful to unpack all the books we have had boxed for so many years... since I now have a place to put them, and so nice just to get rid of the boxes for a change. We are finally HOME... and it feels good. I thank God for all the wonderful things that have come our way recently - after much struggle, the burden has been lifted - I can feel it... God is with us. Fate is finally smiling upon us.

I wish you could be here, physically, to sit down and enjoy it all with me. I'm sure we could talk for hours on end. But as it is, I have to do all the talking (and you, all the listening). That's ok. I know you're here in spirit, and that's all that matters.

I'll write again later. I'm tired. Take care.

Love Denny"

***

It was nice, mostly, just to feel at 'home' again. I spent days slowly putting the house together, enjoying every minute of it. Now that I had shelves in my room, I was finally able to unpack my teddy entire bear collection that had been in boxes for the past six years - and all the books and pictures we didn't ever unpack before.

And I felt LeDon right there with me, as I hung all of her needlepoints and paintings on my wall - without a doubt, I felt her. She is still, always around me... around us. Believe me, she has ways of letting us know:

"February 9, 2001

Dear LeDon:

It seems I owe you a thanks, once again. Kris says you saved his life today... I know, you at least kept him from being seriously injured. When he asked me if he could go brush his teeth, I didn't give it second thought - he's been doing pretty good by himself lately. But as I sat writing, and Sid sat watching TV... neither one of us really paying attention to him, I guess he got carried away playing in the water when he finished brushing. Before either of us knew what had happened, he was laying on the floor.

I had heard a slight bump - the stool hitting the cabinet as his feet left it, I guess - and then he started to cry, just slightly... I looked, to see him on his back, with his head hunched up and his knees bent (almost as if he were being cradled in someone's arms).

Immediately, I jumped to my feet and scooped him up (slipping my hands right through the space already beneath his neck and his legs), looking for a moment, in amazement, at the water which was everywhere... all over his stool, the counter and the floor. I wondered how in the world he had managed to fall from that stool and land on his back, so gently.

As I carried him to the bed, I asked him, "How did you not get hurt?" - and he said, "Aunt LeDon caught me".

We had actually not even talked about you all that day, and to be honest, it caught me by surprise - so I said, "what?" He just stared at the ceiling, raised his right arm, and pointed and said "See, Aunt LeDon's pink and Aunt LeDon's blue". Of course, when I looked at the ceiling, I saw nothing. But I don't doubt that he did... he laid there and stared at that spot on the ceiling for a very long time - and then he hopped off the bed, and went off to play as if nothing had happened at all. He didn't even get a bruise!

It was just as if it hadn't happened at all - but it did. But that could have been a very serious fall... so thank you.

I wasn't sure what to make out of the colors he said he saw... except, maybe our energies really do put off some kind of an aura - and it makes sense that yours would be purple (pink and blue) - I really have no reason to doubt him.

Besides, you, yourself, have let me know you were there before - like the day I was talking to you, alone, in the living room (at the old house) and the remote control truck started driving without batteries. I remember waking each child and bringing them him to see it interact with us. Kody watched in amazement, as it continued to drive around the house, with no one at the control, which was still on top of the microwave because it hadn't been working for weeks. There wasn't even batteries in the truck!

Yet there it was, driving back and forth - and eventually every one of us saw it, even Dad, as it continued to move throughout the day - off and on, as we talked about you. It was obvious you were right there in the room with us.

You always did like to make your presence known... and that seemed just the kind of thing you would do - we were all pretty sure it was you.

You know I've always believed that our spirits go on.... and since your death, that belief has been even stronger. It helps a little, to think that you are enjoying yourself - and maybe that was your way of letting me know that you are. There was definitely an energy, of some kind, in that truck that day and it wasn't batteries!

Then there was the time too, you touched Kristofer's cheek as he played with his Hot Wheels in the kitchen. Sid couldn't wait to come tell me, when, out of the blue, Kris stood up and said: "Daddy, Aunt LeDon just touched me... right here" and gently cupped his hand over his cheek.

Sid said there was no arguing with him. He was positive he felt something, and he knew it was you. I believe him.

Even though we talk about you all the time, nobody was, right at that moment. Sid was cooking dinner, Kasey was watching TV and I was in the room. Nobody else was out there with him. Thank you, for always being here for us. I love you so much and miss you always.

Love Denny"

***

Sometimes it really did feel as if I was losing my mind... writing out bills, I'd screw up on one thing or another over and over. As I'd sit and try to write, my mind would be thinking one thing and my hands would be doing another. I'd try to write 'scooby', and instead, I'd write 'soooby'! Of course, I notice immediately, and change it - but seconds later, as I would try to write out "Gerber Life", I would put a big fancy "T" where the "L" should have been. Next, with the garbage bill, I'll enter it as "water" in my check register... and not even notice until after it was completely written. I just shake my head, and scratch it out.

"February 28, 2001

Dear Donny:

I'm buried in bills right now... too much to do - as usual. I have stacks and stacks of "organized clutter" on my desk (some of the piles I have not looked at in much too long), but I wouldn't know what to do with them at this time anyway. So, there they sit.

I feel a little guilty lately, because I haven't take any time to write to all my friends, to let them know I've moved. It just takes so much time away from everything else I have to do... but then, I always seem to find time to write YOU somehow. I must simply make it a priority, though, soon! It's always a nice break when I make time to sit down and write friends.

I just can't concentrate on the bills anymore, so I had to take a break. And since you are always on my mind, well, it's easy to write you. I need to focus on the many chores that are waiting to be done around the house (not to mention outside) - but sometimes, it's nice to just 'get lost' in my writing... It's kind of an 'escape' from reality, (even though I focus on reality) - and it helps to put everything into perspective.

Plus, it makes me feel closer to you. It'd be really cool, if you could write back."

***

Sometimes it's hard to figure out where your priorities need to be in life, and it helps me, somehow, to prioritize, when I see things laid out in print. I guess that's why I am constantly making 'post-it' notes to myself!

Spring warmed up and things started to get green all around us. It's so beautiful here. I was enjoying being out in the new yard and fixing things up the way I wanted them (or visualized them to be one day) - but I was interrupted regularly with calls from the

elementary school:

"March 12, 2001

Hi Donny...

Just wanted to talk to you for a little while. I've had some

trying moments again lately. Kasey didn't adjust to her new school

very well. The past few months have been filled with emotional

trauma for her.

The school would call and tell me that she was in tears and

no one could console her, so I would go have to drive to school,

calm her down, talk with the teachers, principal and counselor. They

never could tell me what happened. And all Kasey could tell me was

that everyone was making fun of her and the teachers wouldn't do

anything about it. Of course, they denied knowing anything about

her being teased.

Obviously, the kids were picking on her because she was

crying all the time there... but she couldn't tell, exactly, what was

bring her to the point of tears. On that last day, when I finally

decided to pull her out, they had been working on a math paper.

Now, you know that Kasey has always been great with numbers

(after all, she takes after you)... but for some reason, on this day, she got stuck on question #19. She knew the answer - she said she knew she did - but it just wouldn't come down, from her brain, to her fingertips... and she lost it. She just broke into tears.

Then the boy sitting across from her, started making fun of her for crying - then another, and another, and before long, the whole class was laughing at her. The more they laughed, the more she cried... and the more she cried, the more they laughed. How awful for her. The teacher sat her out in the hall, as if she had done something wrong. When I saw that, I was so angry, I withdrew her and told them we would not be back.

I've been researching the Internet for some time now and found out that Texas permits home schooling without regulation, so I made the decision to keep her out of public school. It was one of the best decisions I've ever made, even though almost everyone else in the family was opposed to the idea. Kasey is now very happy, and never in tears over her work... we get along wonderfully and she is learning more than ever.

I am also working with Kris and he is learning very quickly, with Kasey's help. Last night, sitting in bed we were practicing (as we often do before we go to sleep) his numbers and the alphabet...

and for the first time ever, he actually started to "sing" the abc's with

me! In an extremely high-pitched, squeaky voice, he sang "a, b, c, d,

e, f, g, h, I j, k...l, m... and then... I couldn't hold it any longer - I

started to laugh (quietly), and I tried to keep going, but I laughed,

and I laughed and laughed... until I cried.

It was so beautiful! It was an absolutely wonderful moment

that I will never forget. As tears streamed down my face (and I was

still laughing) Kristofer looked at me, puzzled as to why I had quit

singing... he was doing so well, I'm sure he didn't understand. But I

threw my arms open wide, and hugged him, and told him how

wonderful he had done.

I told him he was absolutely perfect... that he had just done

so well, I couldn't believe it - and I was so very happy, it just bought

tears to my eyes. He smiled and hugged me back.

A little bit later, we were able to make it clear through the

whole "abc" song - I very softly, and he, in that squeaky little

voice... oh - so beautiful.

Oh yeah... I received a card in the mail last week, that said

Felix had tried to send us a package - at our old address - but by the time I got the card and called to check on it, the package had already been returned. I called the place that shipped it, but they wouldn't give me Felix's information... so they took mine and said they would have him call me. I hope he does. It's been well over a year since I last heard from him.

Well, I better go. It's late - I should sleep sometime.

Love, Your Lil Sis... Dennel"

***

When Felix did actually call me, it was a bit of a shock. I was thrilled to hear from him, of course, but was really disturbed by some of the things that he told me. He had mentioned, briefly last year, that he had 'become an Atheist' - but I didn't know then how seriously I should take him.

He embellished now, telling me how he was teaching the boys to 'think for themselves' - to 'question everything - believing nothing'.

He has told them that he doesn't believe there is any such thing as a spirit or soul... and that when people die, they are just 'gone' - that we simply cease to exist. He told them my sister just *wasn't* anymore, as if she never were. He is teaching them that to believe in something you cannot see, is just not "logical."

How would I ever reach them now?

"May 30, 2001

Oh, LeDon...

How I wish I knew what to do now. I wrote to Felix and told him how happy I was to hear from him - that it was wonderful to know that they were all ok - but I had to admit that it hurt to hear him say all of those things.

I asked how he could just 'take away' Christmas and Easter, and Halloween... how he felt that was fair to the kids.

I told him I was curious about why he felt the way he did... and wanted to know what ultimately brought him to those conclusions, that nothing after this life exists.

I just couldn't conceive, how, after being raised by such faithful Catholic parents, he could completely turn his back on God... but I told him that I honestly did want to try to understand his point of view.

That opened the door to a discussion about life, which has lasted the past three months. I've explained what I thought it was all about, and why I assert that it is rational to believe in a greater power we cannot see - and he tried to explain to me why, although he once agreed with me, he has (since marrying Tanya and taking Philosophy classes) changed his mind about it all.

Of course, he balked at everything I had to say - no matter how strongly I made my point - and his letters eventually became very confusing to me... full of rambling and non-sense. Each letter became harder and harder to answer... and the last one I received was so harsh, I didn't know quite how to respond, so I haven't yet.

Things have gotten a little out of hand. He actually went so far as telling me he didn't want me talking to the kids anymore, because he was afraid I was going to frighten them by telling them you were still 'floating around' somewhere, watching them.

I didn't want to make things any worse, so I determined it was best, for now, not to reply. I decided to take some time to think about how I am going to answer him before I respond. I've even pulled out my bible, which was in a box in the closet (which I had only looked at a few times before, in Sunday School class).

I guess, it's my hope that the answer is *in there* somewhere. I began with the book of Genesis... and it intrigued me in a way that

I could never have imagined.

I have found myself picking it up, at every slacking moment - even if I just have a minute or two - grabbing my pen and marking through the scriptures. Yes, I marked, with a pen, in my bible... I have underlined, and circled and read again, every single scripture that holds any meaning for me - either that which I understood fully, and thought I might want to reference again, or that which I did not understand and wanted to learn more about.

I'm going to read the whole thing... I don't care how long it takes! And I am going to prove to Felix, somehow - some day - that he is wrong about you. The boys will know you. That's a promise. Until later...

Love always, Denny"

***

Chapter 19

TOUCHED BY GOD

Those letters from Felix... they really got to me. I was so unsure how to answer for so long. For almost three full months, I held them, and read them, and read them again - and I marked upon them as well, everywhere there was something I needed to address. I could even recite them, in part. I let Felix's words become a part of me... and an integral part of my spiritual growth.

Mother's Day came and was kind of strange, in a wonderful sort of way. We stopped by my mom's that afternoon, bringing steaks with us, to barbeque. Mom was in an exceptionally good mood - and she invited me up into the attic - asking me if I would like to take some of LeDon's things home, to give them 'a place' to be appreciated again.

She actually said that she thought LeDon would probably be happy to know that they were being used and looked at again, and that she's probably been pretty upset all this time, knowing that they have been stuck in the attic for the last five years.

It was nice to hear Mom speak of LeDon that way again, as though she knows she still has feelings.

I guess she has finally accepted what is, and I don't have to worry about her anymore. It's a good thing, because I have lots of other things to worry about.

Earlier this year, we found out that we also have septic problems here and the new house (ironic, isn't it?). Soil testing shows we have 80% black clay... so the county won't allow the septic to simply be repaired - we have to put in a new 'above-ground' system.

On top of that, we have recently noticed that the doors aren't shutting right now, and certain walls have shifted and cracked. It is apparent that we have foundation problems here as well. It figures.

***

"July 1, 2001

Hi Donny!

Its Kristofer's 3rd birthday! We had a lovely day, with lots of presents and fun... broke two piñatas - and ate three cakes (one for a friend) - celebrated Kody's birthday as well, since they will be busy at Ozzfest on July 5th (that was Kody's present from Sid).

I've been enjoying working in the yard and getting things fixed up here. The animals are all so happy. It's nice to have a place for them again."

***

"July 4th

I helped Kasey set up a lemonade stand today... she made $11.75! I worked out in the front yard, while keeping an eye on her at the end of the driveway. She had a blast. I'm sure you were watching her too. I was very proud of her.

Oh yeah - and I got a job! I'm cooking in a little family-owned Mexican restaurant just down the road from us. It's pretty cool. I started about a month ago.

Aki, my Japanese lady-friend, called me one morning, as I was getting ready for work. She asked what I was doing and I told her, 'getting ready to go to work'. She said 'Ok - I talk to you later' - and hung up.

I was furious with her two days later, when she called to tell me she was at another friend's house because she had gotten hurt.

That morning when she called, she was lying on the floor... she had fallen out of her bed, and fractured her back in two places!

But she didn't say anything about it after I told her I was leaving for work, because she didn't want to bother me. I couldn't believe it. I told her that I would have called into work in a heartbeat, had I known she needed me... and they certainly would have understood. I explained to her that she means more to me than any job - and she better tell me the next time she needs help.

Each time I called to check on Aki at Kim's house, she sounded worse. She was in more pain every day, and nothing was being done to alleviate it. Kim was always gone somewhere - Aki never knew where she was or when she'd be back and there was never anything in the house for Aki to eat... I ended up taking lunch to her half the time there.

I was also caring for the animals that were still at her house. I begged her to let me come get her that very first week, but she kept insisting she was alright - saying she'd be home in a few more days. But days, turned into weeks, and eventually I knew I had to take charge and do something. Then one night, while up late, writing, my horoscope came through to my email.

I knew immediately after reading it, that God was telling me to help Aki. I had already determined it myself, and now here was confirmation. It said: *"Leo, it's time to take control of a situation that has gone on much too long..."* I found her a new doctor that very next morning. I called to tell her I had an appointment for her and was coming to get her - and I wouldn't take no for an answer - to my surprise, she quickly said "ok". I didn't even get any argument from Kim, so I knew God was on my side here.

I brought her back to my house after that appointment, and she is now living with us... for however long she needs care. Mom, of course, doesn't understand why I would want to do this - we can barely afford to take care of our own family, she says - how can we take in someone else? But how can I not?

To me, Aki is family. I have loved her for five years... and she has no one else that truly gives a shit.

She came to this land, from Okinawa, when she was thirty-two years old. She married an American Marine who promised her mother, as she lay dying, that he would always take care of Aki. He turned out, instead, to be an abusive alcoholic and a womanizer.

Her mother died shortly after they got back to the states, and she has no idea where her only brother ended up. They were married for thirty years, and she put up with him drinking and abusing her, bringing other men home to rape her... while he had sex with other women. Then they renewed their vows for their anniversary last year - and he divorced her right afterward, leaving her for another woman, younger than she.

I couldn't just turn my back on her, and it's easier to have her here than to be running back and forth to take care of her. I know you understand. I love you, Donny"

***

"July 7, 2001: I took a Xanax last night... and it was so hard to bring myself to that decision. I just hate taking medication like that - but I felt so tense all of the sudden. I realized that my hands were trembling and felt so tight. I could feel my eyebrows pressing toward each other, although I was trying very hard to relax. I couldn't sit still - I just felt like I had to be doing something... I decided to cook dinner, but had to clean the kitchen first, and as I buzzed around, everyone was staring at me, asking if I was ok... and all at once, I realized - I was stressing out again! That is so weird."

***

A lot had been going on again lately... with the septic problems we now had there, worrying about how we were going to find money to take care of it, and trying to fit in work and caring for Aki. I have been somewhat overwhelmed again lately, but have been trying my best to stay very aware of my body through it all.

A few days ago, my horoscope asked me if I had been taking care of myself lately... eating right, sleeping enough (and of course, I had to admit, no).

I finally decided - I better take a pill. I stopped shaking within an hour, and was finally able to settle down and relax. A few weeks ago, I had taken a Xanax (two nights in a row, I think)... because I couldn't sleep - and they do help me sleep. I just don't like feeling like I 'need' to take them. I don't know why it bothers me so bad, but it does.

Also, back in June, I was working on the fence out back, digging postholes... when I brought the shovel up and, somehow, whacked myself in the right jaw - hard! It hurt really bad - my teeth clunked together and my jaw cracked.

The next morning, while brushing my teeth, I noticed that my jaw was now really 'out of alignment'. It looks like I have a 'center tooth' on the bottom, rather than two - they don't line up at all anymore. I knew right then that I really should call somebody... and make an appointment to have it looked at, but I have managed to 'put it off' still to this day... I haven't determined if I should go see my regular doctor, or have a dentist look at it, or maybe a chiropractor?

I really don't know, and I don't really 'want' to see any of them, I guess. Besides, it doesn't bother me that much, most of the time - it aches a little at night, particularly if I lay on that side for too long, or when I am eating if I bite wrong... but I have always had that problem anyway - I think I just made it worse.

It probably doesn't help any, putting it off - like I have done... but I'm not sure what they could do for it anyhow; and I just have so many other things to worry about right now.

I know I have deliberately avoided the issue, because I just don't want to deal with it - I already have so many doctor's appointments to go to with Aki right now... and I just hate doctors so... and they rarely seem to do anything to help anyway.

***

"Aug. 9, 2001

Dear LeDon:

I don't really know what is going on with Sid lately... he has been so miserable. He started yelling at Kasey her first night home from South Dakota (after visiting her dad) just because <u>he</u> told her to go to sleep, and she started 'arguing' (asking why). It was 10:00, and there was really no reason she shouldn't go to sleep, but it didn't need to turn into a screaming episode.

He handed me a bill for CD's yesterday, which he had ordered from BMG some time back, without me knowing, in the amount of $62.00! Then he bitches today about a little lost puppy that showed up on our doorstep, insisting that I take it to the pound because we can't afford to feed it. How hypocritical.

You know, I'm sorry, but $62.00 would buy a lot of dog food. Oh, but... we don't really <u>have</u> to <u>pay</u> that bill right now - it can be put on the back burner - we just owe it forever, that's all. (Fucking CD's).

He's already unhappy about the kittens, I know... we have a litter of six, five weeks old, from a stray that we found just days before the babies were born. I have done my best to find most of them homes... but I just couldn't let <u>them</u> be born strays too - what else could I do?

Now we have to get this female spayed, so she doesn't have anymore unwanted babies... either that, or take her to the pound (where she would most likely be put down, because not many people want to adopt an adult cat).

She is so sweet - we named her Sugar... I couldn't let that happen to her. What is one more mouth to feed, when we already have so many? No matter how little I have ever had, I have always been willing to share.

He knows animals have always been a very big part of my life... and who I am. I love them, every one... they are all Gods creatures - big and small, and I adore them; and they have so much love to give in return. They have a way of getting right down deep inside your heart, real fast - this puppy looks at me with those sweet, innocent, black lab eyes... and I crumble.

She didn't ask to come here, but I believe God brought her to our door. I'm sure someone dumped her because they couldn't find her a home, and <u>they</u> didn't want to be burdened. It's just not right! Why should she suffer because of some asshole who was thinking only of his pocketbook?

We are putting up signs, hoping that someone 'accidentally' lost her... but I know - somehow, I just know, she was abandoned. She has been on her own for a while; her fur is not healthy, and she has not been cared for - (if someone comes to claim her, I am going to question them highly).

Kristofer already named her... Toby - after a black bunny he had, who died last month, and he still remembers. I don't know what to do, so I am going to just do what comes naturally, and take care of her for a while, and we'll see where it goes.

When Sid started bitching about the bills, I told him he could take them over at anytime if he wanted... I am tired of doing it all anyway - I would love not to have to worry about it! (But he has never wanted anything to do with it...) He snapped back that I could get a 'fucking job' at any time too – I guess the fact that I was working part-time, cooking at the restaurant doesn't count because I have had to take the past month off.

Aki was not doing well, until the doctor put her on oxygen last week; and we have had so many appointments and tests, and keeping track of her medication is a job in itself... and she needs to eat regularly - and I have never been real good at scheduling meals (we used to eat at all hours of the day) so that has changed my routine a little; and then there are her animals, which I am also taking care of - two little dogs here, (which Sid also bitches about) and one big dog and four cats, staying at her house alone.

Every other day, I drive to her house and feed and water and change litter boxes, and try to clean up a little - it gets pretty tiring. Fuck, I just remembered that I forgot to even go do it today... God I hope Moose is alright.

I know I don't need the added stress, but she needs me, and they need me - no one *else* wants to do it. I should quit now. I love you so much.

Always will... Denny"

***

This was to be a very strange month.

This particular month, I would experience something I had never felt before in my life – and probably will never feel again - but it was something I will never forget:

"Sept. 6, 2001

Dear LeDon:

I had to quit working at the restaurant. It was fun for a while, but the stress became too much again. I was trying to fit in doctors appointments, schooling and everything else; and the money wasn't worth it in the long run.

But obviously, there was a reason I was supposed to do it. I made some very good friends while I was there, who were extremely supportive of me, and my plight to reach Felix. They were Episcopal Baptists - pretty radical, but definitely behind me in trying to convince him of God's existence. It was a needed support system.

Aki has also been a great source of support for me, in my dealings with Felix... she knows God, although she calls him by another name. In recent days, though, she's the only one (besides Kasey and Kris) that isn't a little concerned about my sanity. But I know you, of all people, will understand.

It's just a little difficult for some of those here, to accept, at the moment that I haven't really lost my mind.

You probably already know, God actually touched me last month. I told everyone about it and, yeah... they think I'm crazy -

everyone, except the kids, that is. But I don't really care.

I experienced the most wonderful spiritual journey of my life! I will never forget it as long as I live - the night that God, Himself, came to me.

I was sitting in my bed, at 11:30 p.m., August 23rd... just watching TV, when a surge of energy suddenly flowed into my toes and through my body and 'thoughts' came flooding into my mind. Instantly, I knew it was Him... and I don't know how to explain it, except to say that His power is strong, and unmistakable. Immediately, I felt that I had the answers I had been so desperately searching for - and earnestly, praying for - for the past six months.

I jumped up and said "I'm ready to write back to Felix", and started typing. Starting with a 'description of the soul' and continuing; I typed for six straight days, stopping only to feed my animals and care for my children.

I had been praying so many times a day lately, that I hadn't even been able to keep count - (and yes, I did actually used to keep count). And I mean, I had been 'really' praying... talking, meditating, and listening - the whole bit; so much more than my usual, casual, everyday talks with God which I have enjoyed my whole life. I believe He has spoken to me before, but, not like this... on this particular night, He actually answered my prayers with such forcefulness, that I 'knew' it was Him, without a doubt. It was an overwhelming feeling - to be engulfed by His essence - to be warmed by His love... and He abounded in me, for some time.

I sat, with my bible spread out on my desk, and Felix's letters, all in my hand... and I searched the scriptures for answers - and God led me to them.

Just as I looked for one scripture, another would be shown to me, with even more meaning, on the very topic I was researching - for Felix posed to me, in his last letter, some very challenging questions, which required great depth of thinking - and I didn't know, at first, where to find the answers. But now, as God told me where to look, I found every answer I needed. He explained to me, things like the creation, in simple terms - and the misconceptions of men, regarding it... and then revealed scriptures to me, that backed this explanation. Soon, I had put together a writing, which poses the theory that Evolution and God, indeed, go hand in hand.

He gave me the basis for other writings as well, on things such as Astrology and Spiritual Gifts, and the question of whether or not, animals too, have a soul... all of which were questions Felix had specified.

I sent Felix a package that must of been at least an inch thick. Unfortunately, his response was not quite what I had hoped it would be, but I did get Tanya to admit that she honestly couldn't say "there is NO God" - just that she isn't sure. She claimed that being Atheist does not necessarily mean they 'deny' the existence of God, only that they 'lack a position' on the subject. I think, technically, that's Agnostic... but either way, it makes me feel a little bit better, I suppose. The boys will know the truth one day.

Well, that's it for now. Thanks for always listening.

Always and Forever,

Your little sister, Dennel"

***

Felix and I spent just another week sending emails back and forth. We discussed many different things; but somewhere along the way, I apparently offended him. I had asked about seeing the boys - possibly having them come here to visit - and he said no.

Because of my strong conviction toward God, and my steadfast belief that LeDon's spirit still exists and is close by us, he decided to end our conversations altogether.

I think I got a little 'too close' for their comfort, to the truth. They'll understand one day. And I'm sure the boys will be ok - I'm trusting that they will find their way.

God will find a way to reach them eventually... or my sister will. There are far too many people questioning faith now. The topic is going to be discussed and as the boys grow; and they won't be able to help but face it for themselves.

I have a good feeling about this - the questioning of faith is not a bad thing. It's a good thing because it opens the channels for communication, both in this world, and the spiritual one. Yes, We certainly live in a changing world... and, hopefully, we can keep changing it, for the better.

***

Chapter 20

A CHANGING WORLD, INDEED

Then, in an instant, everyone took notice. Something happened that I never would have imagined - but, somehow, was not that surprised by... "9-11":

"September 11, 2001

My Dear LeDon:

Can you believe the devastation of this day? It seems as if I am stuck in the middle of a bad dream - no... more like a nightmare. At 7:45 this morning, an airplane, full of people just flew right into the North tower of the World Trade Center in New York City! It was thought, at first that it might have been an accident, but very soon we all learned otherwise.

As we stood there, watching the blazing inferno on live television... another plane flew into the South tower. Happening right before our eyes, it was still unbelievable. I had been watching the Today Show - with my favorite girl, Katie Couric - when they cut to live coverage of 'breaking news', just as it happened... it was all so unreal. Both towers collapsed to the ground within 45 minutes

of being struck. An estimated 5,700 people died under the rubble (of

course, they have only just began to take count of everybody that got

out. It could be worse. Given the fact that tens of thousands of

people, are in and out of those buildings everyday, and so many

more are usually already there by that time, I'd say, we were blessed.

It had to be by God's grace that so many people were

detained for one reason or another that day - the stories were endless,

of workers who were held up by traffic... or hung up dropping their

children off at school. There were many who just could not make it

into work in time.

On any other, average work day, there were at least 20,000

people in those two buildings at that very hour... so why weren't

they there, on that fateful day?

Within just one hour of this awful incident, another hijacked

plane flew directly into the side of the Pentagon, in Washington,

D.C. and collapsed a portion of that building as well. They thought

at first, as many as 800 would be dead there - turned out, less than

200 were even in the building at that moment. Another blessing.

A fourth plane, crashed in Pennsylvania - overtaken by its

passengers, after they heard what had happened to the other planes and learned of the hijackers plans. That plane, was believed to be headed for the White House. A threat had been called in there, it had been evacuated - the government too cover in some underground military base for a while and they 'hid' the vice-president... crazy. It almost seemed like the end of the world. Now they know that the planes were all taken by a group of terrorists... the President said it was a deliberate declaration of war against the United States of America. The news is now referring to it as the "Attack on America" - and there is no doubt, this day will live in infamy.

Life is really something, isn't it? Never a dull moment. How many people have lived through the turn of a new century, a new millennium... and a war?!

It's 9pm, almost twelve hours since this whole mess began. Six people were pulled from the rubble earlier today, and they just found two more alive. It's a miracle anyone survived this... those buildings were so huge! But, somehow, a number people did get out of the buildings, even as they were falling - over 100 ended up in the hospital. Over 300 firefighters and police officers were in the buildings, helping people find their way out, still, when the buildings fell. They willingly gave their lives, trying to save as many others as they could before it was too late.

There really is 'no greater love, than that a man lay down his life for another'. God bless all those men. One survivor told the story of his escape from the 80th floor... sobbing, as he explained how, when the first plane hit the other tower, they were all told to start evacuating - and as they reached the 5th floor, they were told everything was ok and they could go back. He said that something just didn't feel right... and he hesitated for a moment or two - and then, at that very moment, the second plane hit, the 80th floor. He wept as he thought of those people who had started evacuating the 110th floor earlier, as they would been on that floor then.

Another woman told how she was trying to get down from the 76th floor of the first building. She said she cold hardly breath, as she suffered from asthma, as the smoke was so thick - and she told, how all she could keep thinking was that she couldn't collapse, because everything was so dark, no one would ever find her... what a horrifying feeling that must have been. I can only imagine the fear.

On the radio, another man told how he escaped from the 30th floor of the first building... feeling the hit, they thought it was an earthquake - so they started heading to the lobby. It took them approximately 20 minutes to get gown the stairs, and that's when the second plane hit the other building. He said as they started heading out the door, the plane smashed into the tower and glass, fire and bodies started falling down in front of them.

They all ran back into the building. After a few moments, the firefighters yelled 'all clear' and they all ran - just ran... he said he ran for 3 miles to his car and never looked back. After he got home, his neighbor came over to wait for her husband, who also worked in that building. I wonder if that man ever made it home? I never heard.

And when I think of all the children that lost their parents today, it makes me cry. I hurt for them - and I am praying for them, because they will have the hardest lesson to learn... just as Erik and Kory have had to do, they will have to learn to be strong in spite of the suffering. God bless those children too.

Well, I imagine you guys have your hands full up there today - so I'll let you go now. I will love you forever.

Your sister, Dennel"

***

There was so much debate about whether or not we should have gotten into this war. Some people aren't even sure we are fighting the right enemy. But, this war was not just about the attack on our people, on our soil - that's just what got our government motivated enough to get involved in it.

It probably happened because those poor people, the civilians in Afghanistan, needed us. Forced to live under the rule of the radical Taliban for so many years now - they had no other hope, without us. I think we were meant to help them.

It was circumstance that brought about our involvement... God, in His infinite wisdom, found a way to bring them help - even though it took a great sacrifice to get our attention. I'm sure He felt it was worth it to open our eyes. Those that lost their lives that awful day served a greater purpose, and I'm sure they have been rewarded for their sacrifice.

Those people are in a better place now. It is we, who were left to witness and clean up the mess, who are forced to deal with the aftermath and learn from it. Life goes on... and we must go on, doing our best to help one another.

This tragedy became a lesson in compassion and charity, as it affected everyone, all across the nation:

"Oct. 1, 2001

Dear LeDon:

It's amazing, what has become of this already. People have come together in the past few weeks, giving so much of themselves... not only financially, but physically, emotionally and spiritually.

People are praying everywhere - they even prayed on the steps of the Pentagon the other day - and it's a wonderful sight. What a good feeling it emits.

People are doing everything they can to help, whether it be giving blood or money, or searching for the lost and missing... it made me so proud to be an American.

But you know, other than the fact that we are lucky enough to have a government that believes in individual rights and responsibilities, we really are not so different from others.

Everywhere around the world, people believe in God (even if they have a different name for Him) - few don't believe - everywhere around the world, people are just trying to raise families and simply survive.

Since we have been blessed with a richer economy than most other countries, it only makes sense that we step up and offer our assistance. We have more material things, and more ability to give... so we should. Knowing that God watches over every one, everywhere in the world - whether they are born into riches or poverty, I believe it is our duty. We are all here for the same reason... to live and to learn.

We have always become stronger, as a nation - and as people of God - after overcoming tragedies like this. History is full of such tragedies, and ultimate, triumphs. I don't know. I guess it's just the way it's supposed to be, even though it all seemed so senseless at the time. I'm going to bed now. I love you.

Love, Denny"

***

As horrible as those events were - and as hard as it is to loose someone you love, we have know... it does all serve a greater purpose. Strange as it seems, suffering is a good thing. It is good for the soul, because it helps us to become stronger spiritual beings and teaches us to appreciate the things we have here.

But the most important lesson to learn, is that death, is just a part of life - the last part - and 'life', as we know it, is just a small part of our total existence.

I believe our souls go on. Reincarnation makes total sense to me... each life, a lesson - and Hell, more a state of mind, than an actual place (unless, this is it). With this world representing our punishment, wherein we learn from our past mistakes - the physical Hell - then death would be our salvation.

Those that we have lost, are in God's loving arms now - feeling no more pain or sorrow. They are gone from this world, but not gone from us. They are a part of us, in spirit... angels, watching over us, until we meet them again.

***

Chapter 21

ACCEPTING 'WHAT IS'

I'm not sure how many of you will know who John Edward is, but he is a "medium" who used to have a show on television and I think he is absolutely wonderful.

Watching him, somehow, fills me with such an inner peace - the man is so incredible, and so lucky to have such a wonderful gift.

He started one night, by getting a message about "the tap dancer" - and after talking to one girl, who was a tap dancer in college, he mentioned an "r" name with a vowel in front - (not feeling that the message was for her) - turned out, it was for another lady, whose daughter had taken tap dance lessons... and had passed away at a young age. Her mom had buried her with one of her tap shoes (and John knew this).

She brought through other spirits who had messages for those sitting next to her mother... one of them gave a description of a house, and told John to "go into the bathroom, and look on the right"... he described a vanity, with a picture on of Mickey Mouse on it, and told of a ring that was missing (the ring had significant value to this person). He told them where to find it.

Another man, whose mother had died when he was a young boy, some 30 years ago... was brought to tears, when John told him that he was being told "the child could not have done anything." The man told how his mother had taken him to the toy store, and when they walked in the store, she said 'I feel faint' and she collapsed - she had a heart attack right there - as a boy, he always felt guilty, because they were there to buy him a birthday present; and the man had felt this guilt his entire life... until he heard John say those words.

If one cannot see the wonder in those works, then they are truly blind... John Edward has a special gift - that comes from God - the ability to communicate with the other side. The "discerning with spirits," as it's referred to in the bible, is, a 'spiritual gift'... one of many that God bestows upon each one of us. Some have this, psychic-medium ability; others, the gift of magic, or of healing... and still others, have the 'gift of faith' (that 'inborn' knowledge, that God exists... such as I was blessed with).

I am currently in the process of trying to find out how to

become an 'ordained minister,' (of non-denominational faith). I

have always 'known' God, but He has spoken to me more this year,

than ever before in my life - and it is so loud and so clear -

sometimes, it scares me, a little.

But, I'm sure this is what he wants me to do.

He came to me again tonight... October 2, 2001... just sitting

in bed – strange – at 9:45 p.m... all of the sudden, I 'felt' His energy,

and my heart started to pound, harder and harder... faster and faster.

He said to me... "tell your husband to feel your heart" - but I

hesitated - and He said, "tell him, I am here".

But I was still a little unsure, and a little scared (and in my

mind, I was replying "no, he'll think I'm crazy").

Then, I heard Him again... He said to me, "tell him - tell

him... tell him" and each time it repeated, it got louder. Well, as my

heart went faster and faster, I thought to myself, 'I better tell him, or

I am going to have a heart attack'... so I asked for his hand. I placed

it on my chest – he said, "oh god" (my heart was absolutely racing).

I said, "yes." He looked at me, bewildered; and I told him, quite

simply, "it's Him".

He said, "OK?"... and gave me a *very* strange look - but I

knew, he could see something in my eyes. Although I was smiling, he was a little bit frightened, actually thinking I might be having a heart attack; and he begged me to calm down. *But I was calm...* and I told him, I wasn't the one doing it - and that it was OK - it didn't really hurt, it was just, overwhelming.

As I held his hand tightly to my chest, for about 2 minutes, my heart surged - and God spoke to me (now I don't have to tell everything He said to me, because much of it was personal - just between He and I)... but, He spoke to me, nonetheless; and I listened. I felt Him working His magic inside of me, and it was wonderful - and then, my heart slowed, returning to its normal pace; and I laid back... exhausted.

I don't know what else to say, other than - it really did happen. And I have to tell as many people, as will listen... that God is there - He really is! This is the one message that comes through loud and clear, every time. He is there... yes, He is - He IS there.

Watching Dateline tonight, I was deeply touched by what a wonderful job they had done with the story of "9-11." They had put together all the pieces, of the heroic journey of the passengers on United Flight 93, on that fateful morning.

They told how runway congestion had put the flight forty-five minutes behind schedule, giving many of the passengers the opportunity to call their loved ones and find out what had already happened to the other three planes... and how that information, inspired all of them - everyone of them - to run to first class, together, to charge the highjackers - and take the plane down. They told how the plane had gone into the field from nose, to tail, straight down... leaving only a hole, about ten feet deep, and ashes approximately four inches thick!

There was nothing left of that plane, or those people... nothing, whatsoever - and you know why? Because God scooped them right up. He grabbed them so fast - they didn't even have to suffer... not one of those people suffered - because they had given their lives, to save, who knows how many thousands of others.

Those people will indeed be blessed, and treasured, by God, forever. This kind of love, is exactly what he wants from us... talk about selflessness. There is no better example than this story. For there is no greater love, than that a man lay down his life, for another... and to save one life, is as to save, the world. These words come from God.

After being touched so, by this story, He was not about to let me just go to sleep. Though I had already been thinking, that I should write about it, I was thinking about doing it tomorrow. I was very tired, having been sick this past week - practically unable to get out of bed for the previous three days - but NO... He said, "get up". He told me I had work to do.

I am now wide awake - and it is long after midnight! I am not quite sure, where my writing is meant to go... the only thing I am sure of, is that I must write - I have to tell, what I feel - what I know... that He is here.

One thing I know, is that I would like this to get to all the families of those who died on United Flight 93... for them to know that God thanks them, for their sacrifice - for it was great - He asks them to be strong, and to know, that their love ones did a wonderful thing... the most wonderful thing that a human being can ever do in God's eyes.

And to those two little children, whose mother didn't know how to tell them just 'where' their father was... (just that he had no cell phone in heaven, and a letter couldn't get there) - I want them to know, that heir father was a hero - and he is now, an angel of God...

a very special angel, with very high honors; and he is not very far away!

And I would also like to add, that a letter CAN be received by those in heaven. I would encourage that little girl, to write to her father. It will help her to feel better, and even though the paper may never physically leave her possession, he WILL get the message... and they need to understand that a cell phone isn't necessary there - because he can hear you, if you just talk to him - just as God hears us when we pray; so do those we love, when they are with Him.

Though it is hard, for a while, to accept being 'without' someone physically... (I know), we must remember one very important thing - it is something I heard a while back, on Oprah, from Dr. Phil - and it truly changed my life: "We are not human beings, who occasionally have a spiritual experience. We are 'spiritual beings', having a human experience."

***

When you think of it that way, it makes so much sense... we are only here, for such a little while - some even less than others, but every one of us, for a purpose - to grow, and to learn.

See God does have a 'plan' for us, each and everyone.

Sometimes the course (or our 'path') changes a little, based upon our individual decisions... but I believe the plan, will come together in the end. He watches over us, while we are here, and He presents us with opportunities; even sometimes, difficult situations, and surprises now and then.

Everything that has happened lately, <u>has happened for a reason</u>. It has been a major lesson in unity, charity, compassion, love, and selflessness. As we have all witnessed these past three weeks... when we allow our 'spirit' to emerge, the most wonderful thing happens... we come together. We realize what is truly important, and how precious life is. We realize what a gift it truly is. And somehow, even after a death, we can still 'feel' the love of those we have lost - because love does not die, with the physical body. Love, lives forever - in our soul - and never leaves us. Ultimately, it is this love that can truly change the world.

If every one of us tries, we can do it - even if, only most of us try... (because I suppose there are those few, who just don't and won't get it). There are those who think we are all crazy. Yet, that doesn't bother me, because you know what? A lot of people thought Jesus was crazy too... but a lot more believed in Him!

I am not trying to compare myself with Jesus... although God says, we should all try to be like Him. I am just a mother - who God occasionally likes to talk to. I have known Him my whole life... not through church, or religious training - and certainly not by example - I have just always "known" Him.

I have been lucky, to be blessed with this gift... though, before now, I never felt the need to profess my knowledge of Him, to the world.

Things have changed, dramatically now though... and He has asked me to do this for Him. So I will try, however I can.

Writing is what I know best - it is my 'physical gift' - so I will start there, and see where He leads me. He knows, I am terrified of crowds - and I never wanted to "be in the spotlight"... that was my sister's wish! Not mine.

At the age of 37 years now, and have lived most of my life, pretty much keeping to myself (never having more than one or two friends at a time, being a social phobic). Yet, because of extensive travel throughout my lifetime, and the many opportunities I have been presented with, I have dozens of friends, from all over the states, that I still write to, to this day.

Having been a social phobic all of my life, and now finally diagnosed with an extreme anxiety disorder, I never imagined I would be speaking out for Him. I'm simply *afraid* of people and I don't know why. But then, I hear that a little fear is a good thing, because it keeps you on your toes.

See, I'm normal - just like you - and just like others... and yet, I am different (just like you - and just like others). We are all basically the same deep down inside, yet unique and individual - each one of us special, in God's eyes; and He just wants everyone to know that. He wants us to trust in Him. He wants us to know that He will not forsake us in the end. *There is so much more to life*, than this physical world that we live in, and these physical bodies that we temporarily inhabit. Know this - and learn to touch one another's spirit, while you are still here... get to know them, inside, as well as out. This way, you will never be without them, even after death.

So tell everyone you love, exactly how much they mean to you; and more than that - show them, each and every day. Life is truly too short - but it's long enough to serve it's purpose, whatever that may be for each of us.

***

Chapter 22

A NEW SPIRIT IN THE MAKING

So now, living in a world at war, everyone was on edge - wondering, what would be next. There was talk of possible chemical and biological attacks... anthrax had already made an appearance. Random envelopes filled with deadly white powder, had been sent out in the mail to particular individuals, for no apparent reason. How can people be so cruel? Why must the world be so full of hate? It's beyond my understanding.

At this time, Osama Bin Laden was claiming that he had nuclear weapons, North Korea told us they had them too and we were certain Saddam Hussein did. So left with little choice, due to the circumstances we were in, we also went to war in Iraq (while still at war in Afghanistan).

Our soldiers fought bravely; and footage of the war was all over the television. Little Kristofer watched in amazement as the tanks rolled, guns fired back and forth and as some of our men were carried off in stretchers. It was hard for him, at three years of age, to understand that what he was seeing on the television screen, was really happening at that moment.

We explained to him that it was all the way on the other side of the world, but we were watching it because it mattered to us. Those were our soldiers, over there, and they were fighting to protect us - so that no one else would ever fly another plane into a building. (Seemed a strange thing to have to even say.)

In the meantime, life went on... we had no choice but to accept what was, for what it was, and to face it head on - hopefully, learning from what had happened. Sometimes, in my personal life, that doesn't seem so easy though.

About 6:30 p.m., on Oct. 4th, I started bleeding severely... and didn't stop. I lost massive amounts of blood and clots of tissue (and then, I knew)... I was having a miscarriage. I hadn't even known I was pregnant, but I knew then.

After three hours, with the bleeding not stopping, I started feeling light-headed; and when Sid finally came home - having been at his brother's house, drinking again - I had to have him take me to the ER. Thank God he wasn't too drunk to drive, somehow; even though he was too drunk to stay in the room with me.

They monitored me all night, verified the pregnancy (as well as the loss), did sonograms to make sure there wasn't any thing left to cause complications, and discharged me at 4:30 a.m. It felt like it had been two days already; it was a very long night, and a tiring day. I spent another two hours in the doctor's office the following day, and it was difficult just to move (my stomach was sore from the trauma). Additionally, it all still seemed kind of like a dream; it happened so fast. I was still trying to process it all.

I had to go back the next day, again, to have my pregnancy hormone level re-checked, because the doctor said it was still extremely high after the miscarriage... and if it didn't go down, it would mean that I had a 'tubular' pregnancy, which would have then had to be taken out by D&C. So I said my prayers, and went to bed - exhausted.

***

"Oct. 5, 2001

My Dear Sister...

It is these days that I could really use your shoulder to cry on. Why would God do this to me? I don't understand. Why give me another baby just to take it away??

It just doesn't make any sense to me. But then, nothing really does lately. I must have really freaked Sid out when I told him I was seriously thinking about becoming an ordained minister... his immediate reaction, being, 'don't expect me to come to church every Sunday' (like *I*, myself, have ever gone to church every Sunday). But he's really sliding backwards now.

For the past few weeks, he has been going out to drink with the guys after work, on Fridays - and he knows how I feel about that. We've been down this road so many times before. I don't know why he decided to start drinking again this time really.

The last time he was on a binge like this, was six years ago – (the reason we split up in New Mexico, just before you died). He has slipped here and there... and we have fought about it - and he has quit, time and time again. But this time is really bad. I can feel it.

Last night, as you know, before he got home, I started bleeding. I hadn't even realized I was due (or overdue) for my period… but, apparently I was. Once it started, it wouldn't stop. Within fifteen minutes, I knew I was having a miscarriage.

The strange thing is, just the other night... I heard God telling me He was *going* to give me another baby. I didn't know I was pregnant, but I felt that comforting message, nonetheless. Now, I have to wonder if it was just His way of preparing me for the loss, or if I will actually get pregnant again one day.

When Sid finally came home, I was in the bathroom and Aki told him that I had just lost his baby. Being a bit tipsy, he could barely comprehend what she was saying. Then once at the hospital, all he wanted to do was go out and **sleep in the truck**... so Kasey went into the room and sate with me. Nice, huh?

Beside Kasey, my only real comfort was knowing that you were there for the baby. You know, I was actually ok with it – Kasey and I laughed and talked the entire time they were monitoring me – though, we also shed a few tears. I know it was for the best. Given everything we have been going through lately, now is not a good time for another child.

So now, you have three of mine. Take good care of them for me, as I know that you will. I'll be in touch soon.

Love, Denny"

***

The days that followed this miscarriage were extremely difficult. Sid was cold, uncaring and distant. We tried talking about

it, but it didn't seem to help. So I decided to write *him* a letter:
(To my Husband):

"Oct. 7, 2001 - 5:00 a.m... I have not been able to sleep all night – and not because of the crowded bed, but because of our conversation last night - I see that it didn't bother you nearly as much as it bothered me.

I am glad you could sleep, actually - I hope you continue to sleep well... I probably won't - you see, I just lost a baby, and it was hard for me, even though you didn't notice. It is still hard. Beside the fact that I am hurting, physically - I am hurting, inside - and you don't seem to care; and that makes it harder still.

I don't know quite what to think about the things that have happened lately... the things you have done, and the way you have been acting; and the fact that you don't even seem to realize, yourself, what you are doing - it makes me wonder if, deep down inside, you really don't want to be married anymore. It seems as though you are 'subconsciously' daring me to tell you to leave.

If that's what you want, (to be 'single' again)... to be free to drink, and to party, and to do 'whatever' you want... then, please, don't stay just because you think that I <u>need</u> you.

I told you before, that I never "needed" anyone... I love you (the 'real' you), and I want you (the 'tender' you), and I miss you... the way you used to touch me, with honest desire, not just hormones - the way you used to hold me, and enjoy it... the way you used to share with me, your dreams, and listen to mine - and the way you used to smile, when we looked at each other... I really miss that smile. Instead, you now wear a frown most of the time... or a tense, hardened 'straight-face' that easily turns to anger (and enhanced by the patch of hair on your chin, which even Kristofer doesn't like).

Have I really made you that unhappy lately??? I am sorry... it wasn't my intention. My only desire was to fill your life with joy - the joy that children, and being a family, brings - the joy of laughter, the joy of hope, and the joy of growing old together (we used to dream of that... remember?) Sitting on the porch, at

80, still holding hands... watching our grandchildren play. Maybe

it will never happen - but it **was** always nice to dream.

You know, we may not even have that much time left

(here on earth) - God tells me the time is not far at hand, when

he is to return – which is another thing... I know you don't

believe me (and it hurts). God *has* touched me (you felt it

yourself - yet you are afraid to admit it - you felt my heart, and

you still refuse to accept it)... So, I must have brought that on, all

by myself, I guess - wow - I must have pretty good control over

my body, to will my heart to such an accelerated rate.

Why is it so hard to accept that there might actually be

'something special' about me...? That God would actually want to

'talk' to me... that there might be something I was meant to do

for Him... Why does that thought scare you? Is that, what has

driven you away lately??? I wish I knew - not that it would change

anything - I just wish I knew, if that's all it was.

If you've simply changed your mind, and decided that this isn't the kind of life-style you want to live anymore, then that is one thing... you are certainly free to make that choice - after all, He is the one who gave us 'free will', and if that is the case, I can let you go, without feeling guilty.

But if I have done something, to drive you away... I am sorry - please know that it was not intentional... I have always tried to live my life, as simply, and honestly as possible. When I give my heart, I love completely (right down to the soul) - I can't help it... and I have never been afraid to express my feelings; in fact, I require it of myself - and I desire it, in return... (sometimes, that is difficult for others, and I understand that)... but we (you and I) used to have a pretty good handle on 'sharing' our feelings - and somewhere along the way, that has been lost.

You, seem 'lost' lately - everyone has noticed it... you don't act like you *'like'* yourself anymore, much-less anyone else; and this 'family life' seems like a burden to you now, when it used to be a treasure... (how did that happen?)

Is it really the fact that I don't want to "get a job" that is bothering you – or, is it that I am complaining too much about how much pot you are going through??? It has been excessive lately, and I am sorry that you cannot see it – because that is when it becomes a problem... and we have discussed this before. You have always known how I feel about it – you know that it is a big part of what caused my first divorce (that, and the violence). I was completely honest with you about this from the very beginning, and my feelings have not changed...even though weed is better than alcohol in my book.

Seems like, it doesn't matter to you how little money we have, as long as I am willing to say that you can have a little each week, for a bag... if we can't pay all the bills that need to be paid, anyway, what difference should it make, right? But then, when you run 'short' and I don't want to give you 'just' another $5 to get some more to 'get you by' until your next check... then we have problems – because you can't stand the thought of being 'without'. How truly, truly, sad that is! So try putting it into perspective... and think about this – which would be worse, to be without your vices, or your family?

I am not trying to keep you 'in prison' (as you so lovingly put it last night), but if pot is truly that important to you, and the 'freedom' to drink a beer 'whenever you want' is what you desire... then by all means, go – don't let me "imprison" you any longer – that is certainly not what I want.

What I WANT... is for you, to WANT to be here, with me and your children – for you to WANT to come straight home from work each night, and look forward seeing us – and for you to BE ABLE to be happy, without having to be drunk or high.

I don't think that's asking all that much – I don't think it's being 'unfair'. But, if you do... then we really do have a problem; and it is one that can only be resolved by YOU making a choice – to be 'free' or to be a 'family'.

It hurt me to hear you say that you feel like your life is a 'prison'... but if you don't look forward to coming home each day, laughing with the kids, and spending time with 'me', then I don't want you to do it! I want you to be happy (and though I really can't believe that being free to drink as much as you want, and hang out with your brother, playing video games and getting high, is the road to true happiness... it is your choice to take that road). Now, I am not saying that I don't ever want you to go to your brother's house to 'hang out' – as when you do it, once in a while, it doesn't bother me.

It's the same with everything, the way I see it – when it becomes a 'habit', it becomes a problem. I know, he's your brother, and you certainly have the right to see him - but you see him every single day at work!

We, on the other hand, don't get to see you at work - and we (Kasey, Kris, and I, in particular) look forward to seeing you when you come home (until you walk in the door screaming at everyone). It always used to make me smile, when you call to say "I'm on my way home" - but lately, it's been a let down, because you come in and start yelling about something, or you call, instead, to say you're going to Brandon's... and I just can't take it anymore - something has to change.

But before you make any rash decisions... let me tell you one last thing - I LOVE YOU very, very much - and it will hurt me, if you choose to go.

Though I am strong enough to make it on my own (as I know, because I've done it before) - it is NOT what I want.

I would like very much, to have the opportunity for God to fulfill His last promise to me... though I don't know just when I will 'feel' like having sex again, I would like another baby - your baby - (one that can stay this time). If you think you would like that too, then we need to work this out without you leaving... because I don't want to drag another child into a relationship that I feel is not going to last. I really believed in us, Sid... and I still do

- the question is, do you?"

***

It seemed to help. Sid read the letter and appeared to take everything to heart. And he promised to stop drinking again.

We stumbled through the weeks to follow, trying to focus on what was most important - our love for our family, and one another. For the time being, we were able to talk things through and I felt as though our bond was once again strengthened.

In this past week have organized all these 'crazy' writings about God, into a pretty decent 'book' format - I believe I am going to call it, "Understanding God" (if that title isn't already taken).

I have found several publishing companies strictly for 'religious' material... and my agent said he had over 200 companies that purchase material 'like mine' - so I feel confident that I can make this work.

I believe that God is doing this for me, as much as I am doing it for Him... if my writing sells, it will not only benefit me and the animals financially, but it will glorify Him, and hopefully it will open many peoples eye's and hearts to the wisdom of God.

At the very least, I'd like to instill a little 'fear' in an unbelieving mind, and bring a little extra knowledge to those who already believe, but perhaps don't understand fully.

The one thing that scares me is the possibility of having to face crowds, if this thing ever gets big – you know, if this book actually sells and people like my writing, and I can get a publisher to contract with me to write more.

I used to jokingly say to people, "yeah, I'm going to interviewed by Katie Couric and Oprah someday" - but to be honest, I would actually be scared shitless if it ever really happened.

And see, what really scares me, is that I know God knows that... which is why He'll probably make it happen! To make me face my biggest fear. The fear of success.

I guess we must all learn to face our fears someday, right?

***

Chapter 23

NEVER QUITE FIT IN

Another Halloween came and went, as did another Thanksgiving. However, this Thanksgiving would not go by without incident:

"Nov. 30, 2001

Dear LeDon:

Well, Mom has gone and done it again. She managed to upset the entire family tonight with her cold and condemning remarks. This year, I was sure to let her know ahead of time that Aki would be joining us for Thanksgiving dinner - she was still living with us, after all. It only seemed right. And this year, Brian's girlfriend, Heather, was living with us too.

We managed to get through dinner alright, but the minute it was over, Mom let everyone have it.

First, she told Aki that she ought to just go back home and quit 'living off' of us, because we could barely afford to feed ourselves... and then she told Heather that she should go live with her mother and leave Brian alone, because all she wanted was to get herself pregnant so he would have to take care of her. That might be true, but it wasn't her place to say it!

I have my doubts about Heather too, but I do my best to try to see what Bri sees in her. I have always told my kids I would support them in whatever decisions they made. I don't know why Mom couldn't ever be that way.

Yes, I believe in honesty... but she didn't have to be quite so brutal! She could have found a gentler way of telling Aki that she was concerned about the financial strain that was being put on our family (even though Aki was helping with groceries) - and she could have tried to lovingly explain to Brian, perhaps alone, that she was honestly apprehensive about Heather's sincerity in their relationship - if she truly felt the need to say anything at all.

But instead, she rudely asserted her opinion and drove us all out of there angry and shaken. None of us even feel like going there for Christmas now and I'm not sure we are going to. Maybe we'll just have it at home this year.

Sid and I are now closer than ever, or so it seems. He says he doesn't know why he slipped back into drinking... the guys just offered one night and, without thinking, he said yes. After that, he found it easier and easier to keep saying yes, and harder and harder to say no.

But after the miscarriage, he started telling them that he had to get home to his beautiful wife - things are much better now. At least, for now. I'm going to try to sleep.

I love you... talk to you later,

Love Denny"

***

When I sent my mom an email a couple weeks later, letting her know that we were going to celebrate Christmas in our own home this year - and inviting her to join us at our place for Christmas dinner - she wrote back and said that she and Al were going back to Utah for the holidays.

And so it was to be a very different Christmas, as we had always gone to grandma's house for Christmas Eve. But we were trying to make the best of things as they were... so we had decided to have a quiet, simple Christmas at home.

Sid and I were still having trouble. It was difficult for him to fight the urge to drink. On December 21st, I wrote to him again:

"OK, Sid. Since you don't 'feel like fighting' anymore, let's not fight... but there are still some things I have to say, that you need to hear: I fell in love with you... because of your soft-spoken nature, your strong, but gentle, touch, the kind look in your eyes when you gazed at me, and the way you used to love me. I meant the world to you, at one time... and now, you tell me you want to look for your 'own place', because you need a 'life' *besides your family?*

You told me once, that I saved your life... that you didn't know where your life was headed. But, you figured, that if you hadn't met me when you did, you would have either ended up dead, or in jail, by that time. That was less than one year after we met. You told me that I had turned your life in a good direction – that, even though you had never 'thought' about having a family before, it sounded nice to you... and, you said that you would be willing to live in a tent with me, if you had to, just as long as we could be together.

Well, we've managed to do a little better than a tent...

because you are making better money than you were making,

when I met you. I am very proud of what you have accomplished

– and I appreciate, so very much, everything that you do.

I thank God every day that I have you, and that you have

been willing to 'take care of me'... that you have accepted my

children as your own, and that you have given me such a precious

miracle as our little Kristofer. I do not mean to take you for

granted, when I forget to tell you how much you mean to me...

but we talk so little any more. Whenever I try to tell you all that I

accomplished during the day, you seem so distant – and

somewhat disinterested. And then I ask how your day went, and

you tell me, 'not bad' – or 'shitty' – but you never really tell me

any details anymore.

You used to be so proud of what you did each day... you

would come home so excited, and tell me what you put here, and

there, what problems you had, and how you fixed it – you used to smile more - you used to enjoy 'just being with me'. On

occasion, if I would be working in the yard when you got home,

you would come and help me, so I could finish faster, and come

in to be with you and we would just lay, or sit together - and,

after a while, we might get high (if we had anything) - and we

used to 'go without', quite often... and it didn't 'used' to be so

hard on you.

It used to be more of a 'special occasion', when we could

come up with enough to buy a bag... and now it's an item on our

'budget'. You complain about never being able to go out and

'do' anything - well, we could go out to dinner once a week, if

you didn't 'have' to have that bag - or go to a movie... if these are

things you would like to do.

I want a husband that 'wants' to be with me - you told me

that you wanted that to be you - that you were ready to 'grow

up' and take on the responsibilities that came with raising kids,

and being a family, just to be with me.

I tried to tell you, right off the bat, that you didn't know what you were getting yourself into... stepping into a ready-made family, and taking on the role of husband, father, and 'provider'.

You knew I had horses, and you stood right beside me every step of the way, in my struggle to hang on to them during difficult times - and you told me, you understood, how much they meant to me. It didn't even bother you that bad, when we were living off of unemployment, and food stamps - and we are far from that now!

I may not have as much time to spend with my horses, as I would like to right now, but that does not mean that they 'mean' any less to me - and I plan to have a lot of time for them, one day. 'We' may not have as much 'time' together as we used to either, but that does not mean that I love you any less. But the desire to make love, lessens, as life gets busier - We simply have a lot more responsibilities now, and you seem to have an 'urge' to be doing 'other things', with other people. I told you, also, when

we met, that I was not a socialite... that I liked staying at home -
and being 'alone' together - that I didn't 'need' other people, and
I would be happy living on an island, away from every one else in
the world. You said that sounded nice, too.

I never lied to you about what I wanted... I still want the
same thing I have always wanted - just to be a mother and a wife,
to write, and to have my animals (and not to be condemned for
it). I never thought that was asking too much - I still don't.

I won't apologize to anyone, for wanting to do what I
believe God meant for women to do... I am glad we live in a world
where women are free to make their own choices - but I like it the
old fashioned way.

The only thing that you can possibly say has 'changed'
about me, is my obvious 'connection' to God... it has always been
there, but in a more subtle, almost secretive, way.

But I can't accept responsibility for that change, because
He spoke to me in way that is impossible for me to deny - and

you cannot ask me to just forget it.

I love you, but I also love God - and I have loved Him, my whole life... I have always felt this 'driving force', which I know now, was Him - He has always kept me focused on what I wanted - and what was truly important in life. We are here, to learn one main thing... which is, that we exist, because of Him. Every other lesson He tries to teach us here, is secondary to that.

We are not here to see who can earn the most money, or who can do the most things or do it better (though some people do strive for that glory) - we are here, simply to 'be', and to learn to be happy with our 'being'.

He wants us to learn, to be 'content' with what we have - what He has given us - and to love each other, and to help those in need whenever we possibly can, not just when we have 'excess'. I truly believe that, with all my heart.

You know I really would have loved, to have lived 200 years ago, when the West was being settled, and families lived off the land, and traded for what they needed, and God was much more a part of every family's life. (Maybe I did live back then – and that's why I feel this way – I don't know, but I have 'always' felt this way.) And I feel very sad, sometimes, because I don't know if you even believe me – that I have actually felt God's presence... And I find myself wondering if you have ever said a prayer in your life (and I mean, besides in church, as a child – I mean, on your own, as an adult – just you and God). Maybe you should try it sometime... He might just be so happy to hear from you, that He'd surprise you, and answer your prayer.

If you truly believe that He is there, then you shouldn't be afraid to talk to Him. Sometimes, you look at me as though you are disappointed, when I want to talk 'about' Him... and I have to wonder, if you really do believe.

I know you believed when we watched John Edward together... that we have spirits and that we do 'go on' – so you can't believe that our existence is merely an 'accident', but do you believe that there is one great Spirit, in charge of it all? And, if

you do, then don't you also believe that it is important to make

Him, a part of your life?

Maybe you're afraid, that if you 'let Him in', you are going

to have to give up pot - well, you don't... He may not 'like' some

of the things we do, but has given us permission to use anything

on this earth that He created –just wants us to use it responsibly.

But, when it starts to 'control' your life... it's the first thing you

think of every morning, and all you think of throughout the day,

then, it becomes a problem.

This is true with all things in life... money... sex... food...

you name it, anything - except God. Everything, in moderation,

is OK - just remember Him, in all you do.

As far as booze goes, though... you also knew, right up

front, that I didn't like it when you drank – because of the episode

at the bike rally. Remember? I told you that I did not want

alcohol of any kind, kept in our house, for any extended period of time. You know I was scared to death by the way you acted at

Sturgis in '94, just weeks before our wedding... when you threw

the snake across the truck at me and said all those horrible things.

I blew it off, as a 'fluke' and hoped it would never happen again;

but then it did – in New Mexico – when you got so drunk, that

you were pissing on the wall right by the bed, and you didn't even

give a shit... and then you scared me to death, again, when you

picked up that knife (to go slash my tires) after punching a hole in

the bedroom door.

So, I think I have a right to be worried about you and

alcohol – and if you want that to be a regular part of your life

again, then you are going to have to decide if it is worth giving up

everything else that you have, because I will not – and can NOT –

allow it to ever get that bad again. And alcohol, just has a way of

doing that... it does NO good, for anyone.

An occasional beer, when we have the money to go out to

a nice Mexican dinner, I don't mind – but going to friends', or even your brother's, and drinking (just for the hell of it)... that I

mind. But I would hope, that being home with your family,

would be more important to you, than having a beer.

I don't think I am being too demanding... but if you do,

you do have the option of leaving, as I have said before. I will not

force you to stay in a situation that makes you unhappy, and if

having the 'freedom' to party to your heart's content, would

make you happier than being with me does, then it is your choice

to make - just remember, that it is not only your life that you

would be disrupting.

Kristofer would not only miss you... but he would miss me

too, during the day, because I would probably have to go back to

work in an office then - at least, until my book sells.

But, if you stick by me - and open your heart to God - I

can promise you, we will have everything we ever wanted, and

more (unless what you really want is to live your life, drinking and

getting high, all the time).

Though you do, I never doubted that my writing would get me, and my family, through our retirement years... and I am more sure of that now, than ever. So please, tell me - do you want 'our' life - or do you want your own?"

***

I'm not sure that letter really made any difference, but he promised to try to do better (again). So Christmas *was* enjoyable. But then that day came once more:

"Dec. 29, 2001

Dear Donny:

Once again the day is here, as the years melt one into another. Christmas was very nice - nothing fancy, like at Mom's, but relaxing to be home for a change. Kasey did all the game planning and led the singing and festivities. She reminded me of you. And Santa had quite a time arranging the gifts in our tiny living room, but the morning was just as magical as ever.

Kristofer is three now, so he's starting to get the hang of it and it was so much fun to see his face as he went through all of the presents one by one. There was no hassle getting every thing boxed back up and hauling it home and it was wonderful to just clean up the mess and be one with it that day.

I wrote Mom today and asked her if she would come over for Kasey's birthday party tomorrow night. She said she would. Said she had a nice time in Utah and had pictures she wanted to share with us. No apology offered, of course - but I didn't expect it. I did note a bit of humility, though. I think we'll be ok. I know she always means well. It's just that she has always had a hard time expressing her love for us.

It's no wonder we were so confused. She sent so many conflicting messages. No matter how hard I tried, I never could understand how she could spank us so harshly and say 'I'm doing this because I love you' - it just didn't make sense to me.

Remember the rubber spatula? That was her favorite beating tool... of course, if that wasn't handy, a strong ruler would do. And somehow, she convinced herself that she was doing us a favor... reciting things such as 'you'll thank me for this someday' and 'I'll teach you to talk back to me' - with an occasional, sympathetic 'this hurts me more than it hurts you' (but not too often) - and it seemed, there were always the same number of swats as there were syllables.

You recall? I remember crying for hours sometimes.

I still giggle about the last time she ever spanked me and the rubber tip of the spatula popped off and went flying across the room. I fell down laughing, which only made her angrier, as she shrieked 'don't you dare laugh at me' - waving the empty spatula handle around in the air. She didn't know what to do, so she did nothing, and never spanked me again.

Well, I guess Mom did the best she could with what knowledge she had, so I don't hold anything against her. After all, everything she did, made me the person I am today - and I like the person I've become... so how can I complain?

It's funny. I always felt like such a *nobody* growing up - and yet, somehow, I knew that I 'was somebody' - always, having this inner peace... a connection to something I couldn't explain. Now, I understand. It all makes sense, why I never quite fit in.

I sure miss you..."

***

As a young child, I was skinny and scrawny. My mom gave me the nickname, Scooby Doo - and I truly never quite fit in. I was the one that nobody wanted, when we picked teams for kick ball at school. I was the one sitting in the corner - lost in my own thoughts - the one nobody really paid attention to.

It's hard to believe that my sister ever thought that I was the favorite. It's true, my family loved me - I knew that. I was the nice one, the quiet one, the 'good' one... the one that tried not to cause any problems, in fact, I was the peacemaker. My sister, on the other hand, often went looking for trouble (and managed to find it).

Somehow, my sister felt threatened by my presence, because of the love and attention I took away from her. From the time I was born, she delighted in tormenting me - making it clear right from the start, that she was the oldest and she ruled over me - by doing little things, like biting my nose to make me cry (and then, ever so gently, tipping my infant seat on its side) and telling mom I 'tipped over'. This story was also told to me more than once.

It's amazing that I'm as well adjusted as I am. I could have grown up with a horrible complex, knowing the things I knew. But I also always knew, she really loved me. Deep down inside, I just knew it - and I always truly admired her.

I'm not sure why she never felt good enough. She was always disappointed with something, in everything she did. And it was all, always so beautiful to me. She was her own worst critic.

To me, she was perfect. I could never do anything as good as LeDon. I was slower and weaker - I couldn't catch a ball... and I never did get the hang of that piano. I was clumsy and shy (and never did like being in crowds). LeDon wanted to be in the middle of everything.

No. I never did 'fit in' anywhere here on this earth. My thoughts were always elsewhere - in my own little world, where families lived together happily, loved each other endlessly and were content, just to be. I just wanted to grow up, get married and have children - to be a mother and a wife - nothing more, nothing less. I dreamt of a simple lifestyle, in a modest home, of course with the animals... and just enough money to get by on.

My mom always said I had my 'head in the clouds' - and now, that makes me laugh. It's true. I was a dreamer (and still am).

"Jan. 5, 2002

Happy Birthday Sis...

I sent Mom an email today, to let her know that she wasn't the only one thinking about you. She wrote back and said she appreciated that.

I wonder how long she would have gone, if I hadn't contacted her first? Not that it makes any difference... I was just wondering. She and I have had some really hard times these past years. I think, sometimes, that she almost despises me; and wishes it would have been me who died, rather than you. I don't know. Maybe it just feels that way.

You are forever in my heart and on my mind, you know? I long to see you again.

I love you so -

Love Denny"

***

Chapter 24

GIVE ME A BREAK!

Mom and I didn't talk a whole lot for the next month or so. She was busy doing her thing - I was busy doing mine. Sid's boss had dropped our health insurance so I was trying desperately to find some we could afford, but to no avail. The bills were mounting and his checks lately were short, because the weather had been bad and the framers weren't done with their part.

Aki, feeling good enough to care for herself again, had moved back home shortly after the New Year - and I got caught up in trying to do this, and take care of that, again. It seemed like things were started to fall to pieces all over the place (when it rains, it pours, you know?)

I was so consumed with everything that was going wrong, I forgot to be thankful for what was still right. Yeah, we had a few things that needed repair - our house, my truck, our credit (not to mention my relationship with my mother) - but at least we had a home, and the truck was still running for the time being. And I knew my mom would come around... she always does.

We had often disagreed, because she never could understand me - I just wanted to be me - and she wanted me to be more like her. Inevitably, though, we find a way to get past the disagreements, because we love each other... ultimately, that's all that matters.

And circumstance was soon to bring Mom and I closer together again. God really does work in mysterious ways. Do you ever notice, that just when you start feeling like nothing worse can possibly happen to you, something worse usually does? When you fall victim to despair, life has a way of slapping you in the face - reminding you, it could always be worse.

The weather had been warm the last couple weeks, and I had the urge to go do something outside. Kasey and I decided to measure off the area where we wanted to re-run the fence line. Then, suddenly, I felt compelled to work with my stallion.

Blue, who was technically my dad's horse, was now four years old. I'd been messing with him since he was six months and trusted him completely. He'd never given me any reason to think he would ever hurt me. I'd actually had the kids on his back several times before. I had saddled him, lead him around the pen - even sat on his back twice before, myself. Each of those times, however, he simply stared at me as if wondering what in the world I was doing up there, when I was supposed to be on the ground, showing him where to go. This time was going to be different:

"February 20, 2002

Dear Donny... what a day!

I can't believe what happened today... it still feels like a dream. I was leading Blue, with Kasey and Kristofer on his back - I know, it seems stupid to me now, too - and Cyndel startled him by standing up out of a puddle she'd been laying in and shaking, as all dogs do, just as we happened to walk by her.

He jumped... dumping the kids off sideways. Kasey turned, while holding Kristofer to protect him and hurt her arm. I took Blue and tied him to a post and went to get the kids to safety. Kris was crying, but, thankfully, unharmed.

I took them inside and got Kasey an icepack, sitting her on the couch - told her if she couldn't move it in half an hour or so we'd have to take her to the hospital... and mind you, we still have no insurance). I told her in the meantime, I was going back out there, because I couldn't end the session like that - for the sake of Blue's training, I had to get on him now. I didn't want him to think he had done something wrong.

The possibility that I might get hurt in the process never even crossed my mind. I was really not afraid of him - not at all.

When I got upon him, at first he balked, but I managed to calm him down. He had just gotten scared - that's all - he really didn't have a mean bone in his body. He agreed to move forward and took several steps, all the while, putting his ears back to tell me he was not comfortable with the situation. But I coaxed him on, urging him gently to keep going... and, just when I had him headed in a straight line, he decided to go into a bucking frenzy.

I rode him through six bucks before I lost my left stirrup and felt myself slip behind the saddle. With my right foot still in the right stirrup and my right hand still on the reins, I felt my face hit his ass, as he kicked out one more time, and then I decided to jump to the ground.

I never felt him kick my leg... but when I stood up to try to move so he didn't trample me, I fell back down to the ground. Still confused about what had actually happened, I tried again - and this time, I actually stood. But then I realized something was wrong. I looked down to see that I was standing on a stub, not far below my knee (and my boot, with the remainder of my leg and foot still inside) was laying, outstretched, to the left of me - still attached by a small portion of skin.

I looked at it for a moment, in amazement, and then, the reality of what happened hit me. As I shouted, "oh, god, no!" I sat back down, reached for my boot and pulled my foot back around - trying, futilely, to snap it back into place (as if it were a Lego)... but it just kept moving around. The minute the nerves touched one another, it started hurting, but by that time, I didn't dare let go of it, so I sat there holding it in place.

Luckily, I had my cell phone snapped onto my other boot and I called into the house to tell Kasey what had happened. I don't know why my first thought was to call my daughter, but I knew she was going to be furious with me - because she had begged me not to go back out there, fearing something would happen.

It hadn't been five minutes since I had left her on the couch, but I knew I had to tell her. She told me she just knew something bad was going to happen. I told her I was sorry and she handled it very well. She went to look for Brian, while I called Sid. I thought

he might be working close and could just come home to get me to go

to the hospital - obviously, I still didn't realize how bad it was at this

point, even though my foot was wobbling in my hand like Jello.

Sid told me to call 911, which I did promptly after hanging

up with him, and they got there within minutes. Sid was far into

Arlington, but promised he was on his way. The paramedics loaded

me (and Kasey) into the ambulance, after painfully cutting off my

boot, exposing the protruding bone and broken fragments which I

had been standing on, unknowingly, at first...and cleaning out the

dirt, and torn material from my thermals, that was now intertwined

with the shards of bone - and they put my leg into a splint. Kasey's

shoulder wasn't dislocated (thank God) - only sprained.

They gave me 20 milligrams of Morphine on the way to the

hospital... said I beat their record for the most Morphine given to a

patient en route. I had 14 milligrams more before going into surgery

- and having a very strange dream. You know - you were there.

I woke up with rods sticking every which way out of my leg,

both, pulling and pushing my leg together from all directions at the

same time. It hurts so bad! They tell me I will be spending at least a week in the hospital. They have to watch for infection for a few days since it was such a bad break - then they are going 'back in' to put plates and screws in and take the rods out. Fun huh? I always wondered what it felt like when you broke your bones. Now I know.

It was just a bad day I guess. I should have judged things better - should have listened to Kasey and respected the fact that Blue didn't want to be pushed.

Oh well... woulda, coulda, shoulda. I'm sleepy. They've got me on some pretty good drugs.

Goodnight..."

***

"Feb. 21, 2002

"Hey... can you believe they made me get up already? They had me meandering through the halls with a walker - I could feel the rods vibrating against my bones with every hop. It was awful.

Mom came to see me... she hugged me and told me she was sorry to see me like this - too bad it took something like this to get her over being mad at me!

My leg looks really weird with all these rods sticking out of it. The nurses here are very nice and I have a sweet roommate - poor dear - she was in a car crash with her daughter. She broke her leg in almost the exact same place as I did.

Wish you were here, physically... I could use a hug."

***

The first few days in that hospital bed drug on, each one, seeming to take forever, probably because I was drifting in and out of sleep constantly with all the medication they had me on:

"Feb. 24, 2002

Had my second surgery today. It took 4 ½ hours. Now I'm in more pain than I was after the first one! They think I can go home in three more days.

Dad's been bringing Kasey out to see me every day, so we could keep up on her schooling - the nurses all love her. The doctor even let her help change my bandage so she can help me at home.

She's pretty sure she wants to be a nurse when she grows up. But she has so many ambitions, who really knows... she reminds me an awful lot of you.

Well, I'm falling asleep... better go.

Love Denny"

***

                                      "Feb. 26, 2002

Can't wait to get home... they said maybe tomorrow. Still waiting for the pain to subside - enduring the rehab is tough - it really hurts just to put it down. It's so hard to sleep. Can't get comfortable laying on my back with my leg eighteen inches in the air. But the drugs help. In fact, it's time...

                                        Talk to you later!"

***

                                        "Feb. 28, 2002

Ok...

So they are sending me home tomorrow for sure. I'm still in a lot of pain, but moving a little better. We know how to change the bandages now and I just have to stay off of it until it heals. No one is sure how long that will be.

The doctor thinks it will be a long recovery... they said I was missing between two to three inches of bone. What was there, was in splinters. They tried to put it all back together, but a lot of it was just gone.

You know, I've never had a broken bone in my life! But when I decided to do something - I do it big!

Ugh... I'm going back to sleep. Love you."

***

As strange as it may sound, I sort of enjoyed my stay at the hospital. It was nothing like a few years ago, when my children were the patients. Aside from the pain I was in, it was ok.

It was nice to get a break from everything (no pun intended). Sid took over the checkbook while I was in there - I didn't have to cook dinner or clean the house. I didn't have to worry about anything, except getting better. Of course, I still worried - it's impossible for me not to.

I met some really great people there (I had three different roommates during my stay) and spent a lot of time just getting closer to God. Funny how that happens when things aren't going so well. I finished reading my bible during that time - took ten months, total. Even as a child, I felt His presence, tho. He was with me when I rode my horse up into the mountains. I would spend hours talking with him... telling him how beautiful it all was - how much I admired it - and asking Him, what I was supposed to be doing in this crazy and confusing world. He would simply give me a comforting

message, that one day I would know.

He has been there every time I needed. Even times, perhaps,

when I have not deserved it. He has never caused me to suffer

beyond that which I am able to endure, and, although I have

forgotten Him at times, I have never left Him far behind.

I may not have always understood why He works the way He

does... why things happen the way they do - but I have always felt

His comforting, in times of despair.

Through trial and error, He has brought me on a path that has

taught me much wisdom, and anytime I have been lost (and believe

me, there have been many of those times), He would offer me an

opportunity - a chance to improve things... a way back.

He always found me, no matter how far I wandered. He

pulled me up and gave me strength when I thought I couldn't go on.

Whenever it felt like every one else in the world was against me, He

was on my side.

He has allowed me to stumble - to find my own way - but

always protected me from danger... and when my sister died, He

helped me through it. He enabled me to realize that she wasn't really that happy here anyway - and I was comforted to know that He had taken her home.

Now, lying in my hospital bed, I reflected upon the past year in particular.... thankful that I had finally found my calling.

Though, I suppose I won't really fit in as a Minister, either. My beliefs are different from most churches - but that's ok, because I know who I am and where I'm going.

We are only here for such a little while, and the one thing I have learned is that it really doesn't matter if you don't fit in.

***

Chapter 25

THE LONG ROAD

I came home with orders to keep my foot above my heart for the next two weeks - only getting out of bed to use the bathroom, with assistance. It drove me crazy to just sit in bed... how could I do that? The doctor told me that I was probably going to be looking at three to six months before I would be walking again. At that time, that seemed so far away.

The very morning after my homecoming, Sid decided to go get donuts. But seconds after he walked out the front door, he came back in, with a little white bundle in his arms. A tiny dog's head, with a long, thin nose, peered out from under his elbow. It was obvious he had been dumped. He was skinny, shaking and hungry. Sid said, "I guess we ought to name him Lucky, because he's lucky he knew which porch to come to". (I don't think luck had anything to do with it, though - I'm sure God told him right where to go - but we still named him Lucky.)

He became my bed companion. He scarcely left my side.

I hated not being able to do things for myself - let alone, not being able to do anything for anyone else. I always much preferred to be the caretaker. I liked staying busy and feeling needed - but now, I couldn't care for my animals or the kids, or fix dinner or anything.

All of the things I had been laughing about 'taking a break' from just weeks ago, I was missing already. This, was going to be hard for me:

"March 10, 2002

Dear LeDon:

What would I do without Kasey? She has been taking such good care of me - she brings me cereal every morning, makes me grilled cheese sandwiches with tomato soup, for lunch (or peanut butter and jelly... or macaroni and cheese) - and she takes care of the animals, and Kristofer, all day long!

Sid is feeding the animals at night to ease the burden on her. They are working together to keep the cages clean - and everyone is taking turns doing dishes... everybody is having to learn to work together to do all of the things that I, alone, used to do.

Maybe this was a blessing in disguise. You know, I never

did believe in 'accidents'.

One good thing has already come of it... since we didn't have any insurance, and my hospital bill was over $30,000), a social worker is applying for Medicaid coverage for us - they should pay most of the bill, and they put the kids on a Health Plan, so at least they are covered.

Kris asked me to draw him a clown the other day, so he could color it for me - so I did. When he was done, he cut it out and gave it to me. I told him it was so wonderful, I wanted to tape it up on my wall right by my bed, so I could look at it every day - because it made me smile. Now he comes into my room and says, "mom, look at that clown"... (so I look at it and back at him) and he (with a huge grin) says, "I just wanted to see you smile". ISN'T THAT SWEET? He's such a great kid.

I signed up for a correspondence course, on writing and publishing, through the Institute of Children's Literature. They say it's easier to get published writing for kids. Since I've thought about it before, I thought I'd go for it (and hey... I've got the time now).

They claim I will have at least two manuscripts ready for submission to a publisher by the time I complete the course, so we'll see how it goes.

I go back to get my stitches out in a few more days. The scars aren't nearly as bad as I thought they would be.

I have scabs covering the holes on each side of my heal where the traction rod was run through, a small slit right below my inside ankle with six stitches, where they slid the steel plate in and the two-inch mess of torn tissue (where Blue's hoof went through my leg) just above that... stitched as well as they could get it.

On the outside of my leg, I have a five-inch cut where they mounted the fibula plate - it has two dozen or more stitches. Then there's the small cross-cuts where they inserted the screwdriver and the other two holes where the rods ran through each bone, which formed the triangular compression I was in those first few days.

It still feels kind of like a strange dream."

***

This past year had been monumental in life... not only because of this accident, but because I had become closer to God than ever before. What started as a struggle to find answers for my brother-in-law, and turned into a spiritual journey that I could never have imagined. God showed Himself to me.

I felt Him – I honestly, honestly felt Him, without a doubt. He has touched my soul and changed my life forever, in more ways than one:

"April 22, 2002

Well, LeDon... it's official!

I received my ordination papers today. I am now, 'Reverend' DB Tyon. I have no idea what I am supposed to do with the title now, but it feels good. It feels right.

I finished reading the entire bible, in less than a year - and it seemed like such a huge undertaking when I started it. But it is such a beautiful book, (even though it is obvious that not every word of it can be taken literally) – it's an extraordinary collection of writings - which I could scarcely put it down. One passage, in particular, that struck me: *'Til I come, give attendance to reading, to exhortation, to doctrine. Neglect not the gift that is in thee... meditate upon these things; give thyself wholly to them... Take heed unto thyself, and unto the doctrine; continue in them; for in doing this thou shalt both save thyself, and them that hear the.'* (1Timothy, chapter 4, verses 13-16). I honestly felt as though God was speaking to me directly through those words.

If I can help others, by comforting them with my words - giving them encouragement and hope, by sharing my experiences... even if I can help just one person, through a difficult period in their life, by giving this little bit of myself, then I will feel like I have done God's will.

I would consider it a bonus, to know that I helped to bring anyone closer to God. I have lost count of the number of books I have started, and almost finished - even printed off - just to read again, and find need for correction, elaboration, supplementation or revision. I just could never seem to get it right. Now, thanks to you, I at least know where to start. Because of Felix, I came to the scriptures... and because of you, I am going to share my faith (and my struggle) with the world. You paved the way, LeDon... you inspired me to write this book because of the way you lived your life. And I searched my soul, because of the way you died.

You have been the strengthener of my foundation... supporter of my spirit. You are much more than just a sister to me - you are my friend, my encouragement, my guardian and my wings.

Thank you, for everything, LeDon...

I love you"

***

At my two-week appointment, the doctor told me to wait a couple more weeks... after that - a couple more. It had now been three months... and I went to see the doctor again. At each visit, they would x-ray my leg and then my doctor would say "let's give it a little more time". It became very discouraging:

"June 1, 2002

Hi Donny...

Saw the doctor again on Thursday... still no progress. He said he could see some new bone tissue forming, but it's still floating around and not attaching to the bone yet. Another six weeks with no pressure - then we'll check again.

It is so frustrating! I'm working on my correspondence assignments and keeping myself as busy as I possibly can, while sitting in my bed day in and day out, but it's driving my crazy. I look out my window at the back yard, and I want to be out there so bad... I hate making Kasey responsible for all of my chores, and having her take care of me on top of it.

She's such a strong girl, for only eleven years old - and so mature. I really don't know what I would do without her right now.

It looks like we are going to have to file bankruptcy. Turns out, with all my medical bills totaled, we are over $100,000 in debt."

***

Every six weeks, it was the same. I built my hopes up, expecting to see some progress... only to have Dr. Collinge tell me that there was absolutely nothing yet. Another six weeks, turned into another, and another - and another:

"July 11, 2002

Well, I cried all the way from the doctor's office, down the elevator, across the lobby and out to the parking garage. I can't believe this is taking so long! The past six weeks, there is still no progress...not a stitch - those little clouds of tissue that were forming before, are still just lingering - barely visible... obviously not interested in attaching whatsoever.

So I still can't put any weight on my leg. Just have to keep waiting. If we had insurance, he said he would go ahead with a bone graph... but since we have none, he wants to wait ANOTHER six weeks and hope for progress. Lord help me."

***

Weeks crept along. Months added up. Almost six months went by and I was nowhere near ready to start walking again yet. The doctor now told me that I would probably be looking at, at least, a full year to recovery so I resigned myself to a new lifestyle, a much more idle one:

"August 6, 2002

Hi Sis...

Well, I turned 38 today. I am now officially five years older than you. Seems strange... you, will be forever young and beautiful - while I grow old and turn gray.

We had to have Salina put down (you remember, our Boxer/Pitt mix) - she killed a skunk that was out behind our house one day and it tested positive for rabies.

Being nocturnal, it shouldn't even have been out... but being sick with the virus, it was confused, and unusually bold and aggressive. It came right up to the back door of our house, and Salina didn't hesitate for a moment - after one bark, she pounced on it, and bit it in the back of the neck - killing it immediately by severing the spinal cord... unfortunately, I now know, that the spinal cord is right where the rabies virus lives.

The county picked up the skunk, and tested it - and we were told yesterday that we had only two options... to put Salina down, or to vaccinate her and put her in quarantine for 90 days (that meant totally isolated - no attention, no affection, and no interaction - other than feeding)... and if she did end up getting sick, she would have to be put down anyway.

I was also told that the vaccination was not 100 percent effective - and knowing that she came in direct contact with the virus, chances were high that she would have contracted the virus.

Salina had lived a pretty full life - almost all of it, with us. She was given to us at the age of three months, because nobody else wanted her. She wasn't purebred, and she was unusually large... but I thought she was beautiful. She moved from South Dakota, to New Mexico, to Texas with us - and was never any trouble.

She experienced motherhood once, thanks to a stray Rhodesian ridgeback in New Mexico. The puppies were adorable, and we ended up assisting her in caring for them (even bottle feeding some) as she had a little trouble, being a relatively young mother... and because she was so large, she laid on two of them the very first night, and accidentally smothered them - I know she was very sad about that.

She always had a problem with obesity (as she was built like a tank), but she was the sweetest dog there ever was - she did look kind of mean, but there wasn't a mean bone in her body. However, her deep growl and massive bark made everyone think twice about coming near... I always felt safe with her at the door.

I now wish we would have kept the little boy we almost ended up keeping, at least then we would still have a part of her here. He was the last pup of the litter - like her, the one nobody wanted - we called him Spike while we had him... and he was 6 months old before I finally found him a home.

Since moving here to Texas, Salina developed several unusual growths (at the base of her tail, on her ears, and in the corner of her left eye) which became rather large and obtrusive - as well as calluses which developed on her buttocks and elbows; and, because of her weight, would break open and bleed almost continuously. She also suffered from arthritis, and that, in addition to her size, made it difficult for her move around - and last year, she tested positive for heartworm, and has been on medication ever since.

Beside the encounter with the skunk, all of these things, were factors in my decision to free her spirit... if she had been young, and healthy, the time in solitary confinement might not have been such an awful thing - but given her age and condition, I felt that death was the less awful option.

I know Salina has not truly left us... Heaven is not all that far away - but even though I have gained the understanding that death is not all that horrible, it was still hard to come to the decision to allow her to make that journey. Sid, Kasey, Kris and I all stayed in the room with her as the doctor helped her go to sleep one last time - and we all cried (yes, even Sid); she knew that she was very loved.

I told her you would show her where to go, because I imagine it is a confusing experience - and I am sure you were there waiting for her. I picture her now, running and playing, as carefree as a puppy once again... no more pain, no more stiffness, no more misery - only peace and love - safe in God's arms, and happy.

You know, I was watching John Edward the other day and really missing you. Then he started reading this lady, who had lost her sister some years ago, to a hemorrhage in the brain from unknown causes (like you). He mentioned the month of August (my birthday), the month of December (your death) and the month of

April (mom's birthday) all, as being significant.

So many things he said fit us, I swear, it felt as though he was reading me! Then he ended the show by mentioning that what came through, was meant to come through... that the people who got a message were the people meant to get it - and added, that a certain message may have been for someone watching at home. It was pretty cool.

Remember, a couple of years ago, when I took Mom to see him in Dallas? He was so amazing - I don't know how anybody could watch him at work and not believe in what he does. Mom claimed not to 'buy it' but had no explanation for how he did what he did. There were a lot of spirits there that night. You could tell, just by looking at him that he was bombarded with images, feelings and emotions - it was a busy room.

I was really hoping you would come through. I figured if anyone could push her way in and speak above the crowd, you could, but perhaps you just felt Mom wasn't ready yet. And she probably wasn't.

Last night, Kody and Brian came into my room. I was reviewing some pages in my Bible and Kody asked what I was reading about.

As I started to explain these chapters, and elaborated on what the scripture were referring to in them, and began reading portions of it to them... I realized that I was actually performing my very first 'sermon'.   At one point, I was looking into their eyes, and they were completely enthralled by my words... and it felt so good, I can't explain it! I had them. They were captivated.

They even told me, when I was through, that they really enjoyed it. Kody said 'Mom, you really need a whole group of people to teach this stuff to - people would love to come and hear you talk about stuff like that.'

It made me so happy to hear my boys - whom I had neglected to teach about God when they were younger - and who really aren't quite sure what to think of all the things I have told them this past year, tell me they enjoyed hearing about this stuff. They were caught up in my words... and they said I was 'good'.

In the midst of it, I was almost frightened, thinking 'what if I'm just boring them?' and my heart even raced a little - but they listened. I actually made them think about the possibilities. It made me realize, that no matter how scared I am, I could do this. It felt so good when I was done. I realized that I don't really have to convince anyone... I just have to be good enough, to get them to listen. If I can put just a grain of faith into people's hearts - give them some small strand of hope to hang onto - then, I will have done my job. Right?

Sid bought a cake for me today and the kids all came in and sang to me... it was nice. Think I'm gonna try to close my eyes now. I love you.

Forever, love Denny"

***

Chapter 26

A LETTER FROM HEAVEN

About a month later, my mom sent me the most beautiful poem. She said she just 'found' it on the Internet - anonymously written. It was especially meaningful to me, given the fact that I had written LeDon so many times wishing she could write me back and started this book so many years ago - giving it the title, then "A Letter to Heaven".

This poem was entitled "A Letter *from* Heaven", and it went like this:

"To My Dearest Family... Some things I'd like to say, but first I'd like to let you know, that I arrived okay. I'm writing this from Heaven, where I dwell with God, above; there's no more tears or sadness here - just eternal love.

Please do not be unhappy, just because I'm out of sight. Remember that I'm with you every morning, noon and night. That day I had to leave you, when my life on Earth was through, God picked me up and hugged me... and said, 'I welcome you - it's good

to have you back again. You were missed while you were gone.
And as for your dear family, they'll be here later on.'

He said 'I need you here so badly, as part of My big plan.
There's so much that we have to do, to help our mortal man.' Then
God *gave* to me, a list of things, He wanted me to do - and foremost
on that list of mine, is watching over you. I will be beside you,
every day and week and year. And when you're sad, I'll be there, to
wipe away the tear.

When you think of my life on Earth, and all those loving
years, because you're only human, it's bound to bring you tears. But
do not be afraid to cry, it does relieve the pain. Remember, there
would be no flowers, if there were no rain.

I wish that I could tell you, of all that God has planned. But
if I were to tell you, you wouldn't understand. One thing is for
certain - though my life on Earth is over... I am closer to you now,
than I ever was before. There are rocky roads ahead of you, and
many hills to climb, but together we can do it, taking one day at a
time.

It was always my philosophy, and I'd like it for you too, that
as you give unto the world, the world will give to you. If you can

help somebody, who's in sorrow or in pain, then you can say to God at night, my day was not in vain.

And now I am content, that my *life* was worthwhile, knowing as I went, I made somebody smile. So if you meet somebody, who is down and feeling low, just lend a hand to pick him up as on your way you go. When you are walking down the street, and you've got me on your mind - I'll be walking in your footsteps, only half a step behind. And when you feel the gentle breeze, or the wind upon your face, that'll be me... giving you a great big hug, or just a soft embrace.

And when it's time for you to go, from that body, to be free - remember not to be afraid - you'll be coming here, to me. I'll be waiting for you, in that land way up above. And I will be in touch again. PS: God sends His love" (Anonymous, 2002).

The poem was signed, "Author Unknown", but I knew where it had come from:

"Sept. 30, 2002

Dear Donny:

I got your letter. What a special surprise it was! Pretty clever - inspiring someone to write that for you and having them put it on the Internet - arranging it, so Mom would find it that way. Yeah. Pretty clever. She claims, there was no special reason she chose that poem... just thought it was pretty. But I know better. It was meant for us. Thank you. We needed that.

It looks like I am going to have that bone graft after all - it's been eight months now and there's still no sign of healing. I go back into the hospital October 15th for surgery again. Fun, fun, fun.

At least this time, I can prepare for my stay. They are going to take the bone from my hip. Sounds a little painful... but I guess I have no choice.

Later... love Denny"

***

The surgery wasn't too bad - although my hip was awfully stiff and sore afterward. It actually hurt worse than my leg did now. I had a private room this time, and only had to stay three days. I saw a couple of the same nurses who cared for me before, which was nice... but I was glad to get home again. I did nothing but sleep for the first few days home.

For the first week, I was too sore to even sit up. But it only took a couple of weeks to work the stiffness out and eventually I was

feeling back to 'normal' again... as normal as I'd felt in the past eight
months anyway:

"Oct. 29, 2002

Dear LeDon:

I went back in today to get the stitches out from the bone
graft. Now I have a lovely scar right down the front of my leg, too,
to match all the ones on the sides. Kasey was excited because the
doctor actually let her cut one of the stitches, while he held them
with the tweezers and pulled.

Once, I said 'ouch' and he said 'she's not hurting you' - and I
told him, 'no, she's not... you are'! Kasey is absolutely sure she
wants to be a nurse now.

The doctor said to come back in another six weeks.

U-u-g-g-h-h..."

***

It was about this time that I was able to get back in touch
with Felix - and for the first time in almost seven years, spoke with
Erik and Kory on the phone:

"Nov. 3, 2002

Dear LeDon:

It was so nice talking with the boys tonight! Erik said he still remembered me - he says he remembers all of us.

He asked why we hadn't been by to see him in so long... and when I told him we were living in Texas, he seemed surprised, like Felix had never even told him. He actually thought we were still living there in Las Vegas and just hadn't bothered to come see them in years. I assured him that would never be the case.

Felix swears to me that he has given the boys every card and letter I have ever sent, but when I asked Erik if he had received all my cards (and birthday money), he said no. Felix claims he just doesn't remember things like that. I don't know.

I had a fairly decent conversation with both Felix and Tanya. Only slightly heated at certain points.

Felix is still opposed to the boys coming to see us here, but he did offer to have Kasey come out there to visit. So she is going up later this month - maybe over Thanksgiving, to spend the holiday with them, even though they don't celebrate it anymore.

I told her we would have our dinner when she got back.

I'm going to go for now. I'll write again later.

Love Denny"

***

Kasey flew up the week before Thanksgiving and stayed ten days. She had a great time - but it didn't go quite as smoothly as I had hoped it would:

"Dec. 1, 2002

Dear LeDon:

Well, Kasey enjoyed her visit to see the boys, except for the one night that all the kids got in a fight. I asked her to be subtle, if she talked about God at all while she was there - just to enjoy being there and being able to let the boys know how much we love them. Not to push the subject of faith, you know?

But it was difficult for her. She sees Him everywhere too, and sometimes, she can't help herself.

Felix and Tanya handled everything well - and all in all, they had a great time. We did have some trouble on the return flight. Felix didn't complete some paperwork and they lost track of her for a while! Hope he doesn't get in any trouble.

Well, I'm moving around pretty darn good on these crutches

now. They almost seem natural. It's now been over nine months since the accident. By the time I start being able to walk without crutches, I'm going to have to learn how to walk all over again. I think this chapter in my life was a lesson in patience... I never have been a very patient person, you know?

But I am much better now. I have learned so much through this ordeal. I'll sure be glad when it's all over.

I have stayed pretty busy with my assignments from the Institute of Children's Literature - it's been fun and I've learned a lot - plus I've done more writing to family and friends this year than I have in a long, long time. I have come to realize, too, how important that is to keep up on.

Sadly, though, most of our family thinks I have lost my mind. They think my ordination was some kind of joke - because, as Aunt Karen and grandma are constantly reminding me, 'women just don't have the precious gift of the priesthood'.

So, I've been reading the Book of Mormon these past few months (out of curiosity) and I found a passage that actually says that God speaks 'not only to men, but to women also'.

When I confronted her with that, she didn't have any

explanation. I just received a typical Mormon response: 'From the beginning of time, Our Father in Heaven designated the Priesthood to be held by men. Women can get the same blessing through a worthy priesthood holder. We have lady Relief Society presidents that have the ability to discern the needs of the ladies she presides over, and she is set apart by the Priesthood leaders to do that job'. Basically saying, it has always been this way since the beginning of time and it has just always been accepted by the women in the church to be that way.

None of that even makes sense to me! Women are just supposed to believe this stuff because somebody said it has been that way 'since the beginning of time'? The Church hasn't even been in existence that long. And their own book says otherwise.

Given what I remember from our youth, though... women were always put down in the Mormon Church - made to feel lowly and unworthy. But from what I've read so far, the Book of Mormon doesn't really put women down. So its just the men who have.

That's why I left the church though. I couldn't listen to them telling me God would never speak directly to me, because I'm not a man, when I had already heard him! I knew better.

Do you remember when we were kids and I used to joke about having my own church someday? Even I didn't know, then, that I was headed in this direction. But I guess I *knew* something.

I don't actually have plans to start a church or anything - but I'm thinking about what I can do with my ministry. I do believe I was compelled to become ordained for a purpose. Whatever that purpose is, has yet to be shown, but I trust God knows what He is doing. I'm just following His lead.

Mom told me recently that she's not even sure there is a Heaven... she doesn't even know that there is a God or anything, she says now. All those years we practiced Family Home Evening, and went to Sunday School - she was shoving all that crap down our throats and she didn't even buy any of it!

She was faking it, because that's what she was told she was supposed to do. How sick is that? I don't think church should teach you to just 'fake it' if you don't feel it.

It hurt me so badly to learn that she never truly believed anything she was teaching us. In a way, I felt betrayed by her.

I told her I would never teach my kids something I didn't honestly believe myself... and that's why I just didn't teach them anything for the longest time.

Maybe God is using her lack of faith as a means to catapult my spiritual growth, because it only makes me more determined now. One of these days I will reach her too.

All my love, Denny"

***

Even though I was born and baptized into the Mormon Church, I feel (and have always felt) that many of their teachings are just wrong. In a way, it's not much more than a cult - brainwashing their children with made-up doctrine and prepared speeches so that they would act the way they wanted them to act. I figured out before the age of 13 that I really didn't want to be part of it.

But that doesn't mean that I think the basis of the church is false. The church was founded on good principle... it is men that have corrupted it (and I do mean men, and men alone, because woman have no say about anything that goes on in the church).

I have always felt God near me. I didn't need anybody to tell me where He was - or how I should live in order to please Him... or how, or where, I should pray to be heard by Him. So, as soon as I was able to make the decision for myself, I left the church... but I never turned from God.

I simply refuse to be led by others who are only doing what they are taught, *because* it is what they were taught - who follow blindly, those before them… I would rather trust my own heart and mind.

So many things in life don't make sense, because people are just screwed up. But there is so much in this life that DOES make sense... it couldn't possibly be just a fluke.

Nature is too symmetrical, too perfect - too deliberate - to be an 'accident'. In every thing, I see God's careful consideration... His thoughtfulness and fairness in its planning. If you really look, you can't help but see it.

***

Chapter 27

BABY STEPS

"Dec. 29, 2002

Dear LeDon:

This is now the seventh year without you. My calendar will never be the same again, you know? It was inevitably, and indefinitely, altered the day you died. My years now begin and end on this day.

Kasey will be 12 tomorrow. She has grown up so fast - and she looks so much like you. She got your dark, thick hair, your round face, and those beautiful, big dimples. It's so hard to be sad, and happy, all at the same time. So sad, because I'm missing you - but so happy for what I have and how much she reminds me of you.

I went back to see my doctor earlier this month. Finally, some progress! Some tissue has begun to attach to the bone - it's a very thin, cloudy layer, but it's there. Dr. Collinge says if it keeps it up and looks stronger at my next visit, he'll let me start taking a few steps. I can't wait.

I'm getting so frustrated, wanting to do stuff and still not being able to. It's hard to carry anything or move anything or clean anything when your hands are hanging onto crutches in order to stay standing. Right now it's most just the Christmas mess I'd like to take care of.

We have finally come to enjoy ourselves again through the holidays, though it will never be quite the same, without you. You were such a child at this time of year. These days were truly one of your greatest pleasures - decorating, cooking, baking, singing and playing games. But most of all, you loved watching everyone open their presents, one by one.

So we will try to honor your memory by continuing to do all those things that you so loved - reminding the kids what it meant to you. You remain, not only in our memories and our hearts, but in our lives... forever.

With Love Always... Dennel"

***

The New Year brought new hope for me. It had been almost a year since my injury. The doctor was going to start letting me put weight on my leg very soon - a little at a time, he said. Trying to be optimistic, I set my sights on being off the crutches by spring. I worked hard at my physical therapy, focusing on my recovery, while not letting it control my life as much as it had been for the past year. I was slowly, steadily, learning how to do more and more things for myself again; and I was shocked at how hard it was.

I was feeling confident, though, that it wouldn't be long before I was back in the saddle. I was encouraged by little things - like my horoscope that said: "**Have confidence that you are ready for the next major step in your journey.**" (Sounded appropriate).

But I was slightly disconcerted when I read "**You are only harming yourself by pretending that everything is OK if it is not.**"

Sid had been sober for over a year now... and he was trying really hard to do as much as he could around the house when he wasn't working (or at least to see to it that the kids got things done each day). It was nice to have him stepping up and really taking care of me for a change, but it was sad that it had to take something like this for him to want to do it.

After trying to run the checkbook and budget for just a few weeks after my accident, and taking responsibility for most of the feeding and chores over the past year, Sid was telling me how much he appreciated everything I normally do around the house - and that I would never have to work again, if I didn't want to.

It seemed that he truly loved me again, as much as he ever did and was happy once more just to be a family. The whole experienced seemed to bring us all together, as a family, actually. Everyone was working together to help do all the chores I used to take care of... and they bonded - my dad, the kids, and Sid - and finally, it seemed, appreciated me for all I did.

During the months I had left of ordered bed rest, I did a lot more writing and kept close tabs on my horoscope, as it kept enchanting me with things like: "It may be time for you to make an important change in your current attitude. *Embrace differences in perspectives and opinions.*"

It told me to: "*Open up the gates of communication and let the stampede come charging through.*"

I love listening to other people's ideas and started thinking about starting a forum, of sorts, for discussions about religion and spirituality. But is this the attitude I'm supposed to change?

It tells me: "*In reality, this is a message reminding you to think about things in terms of the collective, the oneness of us all. Be aware of a greater perspective in which you see more than just your side of the coin.*"

Ok - I've tried really hard to look at as many points of view as possible regarding creation, evolution and the like... but I still can't see it as anything but a well thought out miracle.

I began getting messages that told me to: "*Realize that some of the most important lessons in life were the ones that you learned when you were six years old.*" It said to: "*Return to that state of mind, and embrace the simplicity of life that you experienced then…*" adding: *Life is only complicated because you make it so. Remember what it was like to live carefree - and live that way again*".

I've *always* tried to do that.

It also said... "*Your job is to infuse a bit of playfulness in every situation. Remind people that we are all on this stage together and that we need to make the most of it, instead of always trying to shove each other off.*" So that's what I have tried to do with my writing and my 'practice preaching'.

I'm always telling people that life is just one big classroom - that it's an awesome adventure, a ride, or a game, if you want to look at it that way - that the goal is to absorb as much knowledge as we can while we are here and just do the best we can with it.

We are here, quite simply, to learn... and perhaps, we shouldn't take everything here so seriously.

Life, as we see it, turns out *not* to be "reality."

***

Chapter 27

TO THE SKEPTICS

I just need to say a few more things here, about "belief" (in general), in response to questions I have been asked by several Atheists - as well as some statements I have found online, made by skeptics as well as believers.

Most skeptics use the inconsistencies in the Bible as the bases for their argument against God, and most "believers" use a denial of any contradiction in the Bible to support theirs (though there are plenty of contradictions in there).

I like to find the middle ground... there is plenty of reason that the Bible can't possibly be taken literally. But that doesn't make God any less real. The scriptures were actual writings of men, much like my own – simply journaling, inspirations, ideas and opinions. These ancient writings were found in various places, translated and bound into the first book ever printed, in the year 400AD, and proclaimed holy by the Roman Catholic Church – and since it was printed in ancient languages, few people could read it.

This fact allowed them to proclaim it "holy."

The first description of the world's creation in Genesis is accurate, with the exception of 'days', being, in reality, hundreds of thousands of years. But that can be explained easily with the scientific 'time and space' theories that now exist - and though details were left out about the process of our evolution, it is alluded to with the statement that 'all things came from the water'.

The story of Adam & Eve, which immediately follows (only because a certain group of men chose to put these certain scriptures together)... is, in fact, an allegory - a symbolic representation, using fictional characters to explain human behavior and existence. There is even a scripture that specifically admits to using allegories in the Bible to explain our human interaction in this physical world (and of course, everyone knows that Jesus loved to speak in parables).

When I say that I have always 'known' God, what I mean is that I have always felt, in my heart, that He was there - I realized, very early in life, the connection between 'instinct' or 'intuition' and "God". He is that voice of wisdom that speaks to us all. We choose to hear him - or choose not to listen... I have always heard him. But it has to be noted that the heart hears differently than the ears.

It is true that knowing something 'in your heart' is not like knowing two plus two is four, but it is, every bit, just as real.

My heart and my mind are inexplicably intertwined - I trust both, equally. But even leaving my heart out of it, the most logical thing I can come up with in my mind, is that there has got to be more to life than this.

If there were no spirit, no place that we go... no life after this, then this life truly would be meaningless. It wouldn't matter what we learned, what we did, who we met, who we loved or what we taught our children.

If we just go into nothingness, and are simply 'gone' when we die, then we wouldn't care if anyone remembered us - if anyone liked us – or, if anyone loved us... and the fact is, we do care!

We care a lot. We crave this everlasting connection. We love, we nurture, we care. So it is "logical" to deduct that we feel these things for a reason.

One popular skeptic, Doug Jesseph, says that the God whose existence he denies is supposed to be a "person"... "to have a mind, will, intelligence, purposes and desires". Well, the God whose existence I *defend* is *not* supposed to be a person at all.

He is a "spiritual being"... simply, an ENERGY - not with a "physical mind" like ours, but - indeed - with intelligence, a will, love, purpose and desires.

For him to say that he is "not interested in debating the existence of an impersonal God, who could be identified with nature, or fate, or any other vague 'something' that is supposed to run the universe", appears, to me, to be a cop-out.

Not even the Bible claims God is a *person*. Quite simply, it says that He IS, always WAS and always will BE… kind of like energy, which, so far as we know, cannot be created or destroyed – only altered in form. Hmmm.

Now the Bible does say that we were made 'in His image'... but images can take many forms. A physical form had to be chosen for this physical world that could allow us to do the things He wanted us to do, and to think the way He desired us to think.

Mr. Jesseph's refusal to debate God as anything other than a person proves that he can find no argument against God being 'a spiritual energy that deliberately, or otherwise, causes things to happen' - and that's exactly what God is.

The fact that "thunderstorms, earthquakes, plagues, eclipses, the variety of natural species, and even the origins of life itself, all have detailed atheistic explanations" (as Doug Jesseph points out on his site), does not in any way mean that there is NO God... it simply proves that people, over the years, have often misunderstood how God works. Obviously, God gave all these things physical reasons for being – a way to evolve, and provided reasonable explanations for their existence - so we could figure it all out.

He gave us signs and showed us how to read them. He gave us clues, to make us curious and encouraged us to investigate. He didn't intend for us to be completely ignorant and illiterate forever - He just couldn't give us all the answers right away. After all, if we didn't have anything to learn, what would be the purpose of life?

At one point, Mr. Jesseph argues in God's favor, as he says "God is supposed to act in space and time, but without have a location in space and time. His essence is, according to the tradition itself, ungraspable and fully beyond the comprehension of finite human minds." He continues to support the idea, by saying, "The moral perfection of this deity will, I think, be easily enough granted. God, as traditionally conceived, inflicts no unwarranted harm and can never justly be blamed for anything."

But I believe he is only partially right here… In my view, as a spiritual being (consisting of only energy and no physical matter), God doesn't need a "location" in space and time. He can be anywhere, and everywhere, He wants to be, when He wants to be. In fact, He can - quite logically - exist in all places, at all times. Yes… it is ungraspable and fully beyond the comprehension of our finite human minds (and that is why He is God and we are not).

In order to even begin to comprehend Him, you have to comprehend your own spirit first. So, of course, if you don't even recognize that you HAVE a spirit, it would be difficult, at best, to feel His essence.

I have a different point of view about God's culpability where our trials and tribulations are concerned though (and it's not really in God's favor). I think it's incorrect to believe that He never inflicts unwarranted harm and can never be justly blamed for anything. I blame Him for a lot, actually.

The Bible is full of stories in which God speaks to certain men, telling them to go forth into new lands and conquer certain cities - giving details about the city and the people in it - and He tells these men that they should slay 'everyone' in the city (including women and children), indicating that if they didn't, these people would "be a thorn in their sides", because they would continue to "do evil things"... even though the women and children hadn't really done anything at all.

I don't think we are supposed to fully understand it. But, maybe - just maybe – if there is any truth to these stories, God didn't see anything 'morally' wrong with taking all those innocent people because it doesn't *really* matter how long we are here (since there IS something after this). Maybe, too, that something more is even better than this. Maybe, all that really matters is what we learn while we are here, and what we teach others.

It is completely logical to assume that we are here to learn something... to assume that life has a lot to teach us... *and* to believe that life is more than a mere accidental, singular existence. If that's all it was, the only thing that would matter would be how long we survived - it wouldn't matter what we accomplished, or who was in our lives - because the minute it was over, it would all mean nothing. And how sad is that?

What a gloomy outlook to have on life.

Perhaps Felix is right, in that, most people probably just

'choose' to believe in God simply because it gives them something to hope for. But that doesn't make Him any less real. And what's wrong with a something to hope for, anyway?

Regarding 'other gods', Mr. Jesseph claims "believers must hold that all other deities are illusory, and that people who believe in them are in the grip of a massive error". Not true. I argue that God is god to all people, regardless of how they see Him.

I think He has represented Himself differently, to different people, at different times, depending upon their culture so that they could more easily understand or accept Him, (or perhaps, even to deliberately cause confusion, as another test for us). But ultimately, He wants us all to come to know Him, however we can. It doesn't matter how we perceive Him.

Even "new age" doctrines and the healing power of crystals, which Mr. Jesseph claims 'most believers use a double standard to debunk', I see as God's work too. Just one of the many ways I believe He has chosen to connect with us, like Astrology and other ancient doctrines as well; and it angers me that churches call it the devil's work.

I wish I could help the indoctrinated realize that God exists outside of church. If every organized religion could just accept that they are not all that special - and that none of them have it all right - and that they aren't the only ones that will "get into Heaven", we'd all get along much better. I want to lead people to that middle ground.

Mostly, I wish I could help the skeptics to see what I see... that there are far too many coincidences in this life for any of it to be a coincidence - that there is too much perfection for it to be a mistake. There are too many consistencies in structure and function, within every single life form, for it to be anything but a carefully orchestrated, well thought-out plan. So I think they should at least give God the benefit of doubt.

I really don't think God cares what you label yourself, or how you believe, as long as you treat others kindly and love with an honest heart. If we could only all agree that those things just don't matter, the world could be a much better place.

It is my hope that this book will bring peace to some and understanding to others.

***

(TO BE CONTINUED)